W9-BRL-498

JEWELRY

Upcycled!

Recycled Plastic Bracelet by Steven James

JEWELRY
Upcycled!

TECHNIQUES AND PROJECTS FOR
REUSING METAL, GLASS, PLASTIC,
FIBER, AND FOUND OBJECTS

POTTER
CRAFT

New York

SHERRI HAAB
and MICHELLE HAAB

Photos on pages iv, vi-vii, 9, 10 (left and middle right), 18 (left), 34, 40, 44, 50, 55, 56, 63, 65, 70, 76 (left and top right), 80, 90, 96 (left and bottom right), 100, 105, 106, 109, 112, 118 (left and top right), 122, 127, 128, 132, 136, 139 (bottom), 143 by Zachary Williams / Williams Visual © 2011 Random House, Inc.

Illustrations on page 62 by Laura Polley

Published in the United States by Potter Craft, an imprint of the Crown Publishing Group, a division of Random House, Inc., New York.

www.crownpublishing.com

www.pottercraft.com

POTTER CRAFT and colophon is a registered trademark of Random House, Inc.

Library of Congress Cataloging-in-Publication Data

Haab, Sherri.

 Jewelry upcycled! : techniques and projects for reusing metal, glass, plastic, fiber, and found objects / Sherri Haab and Michelle Haab.

    p. cm.

  Includes index.

  ISBN 978-0-8230-9990-0 (alk. paper)

 1. Jewelry making. 2. Found objects (Art) I. Haab, Michelle. II. Title.

  TT212.H35 2010

  745.594'2--dc22

                              2010034124

ISBN 978-0-8230-9990-0

Printed in China

Design by Jane Archer (www.psbella.com)

10 9 8 7 6 5 4 3 2 1

First Printing, 2011

Dedicated to those who encourage children to be
creative even when glue is spilled, beads are scattered,
and art projects remain unfinished.

ACKNOWLEDGMENTS

Thank you to our family—Dan for helping us with photos and technical questions, for supporting us through late nights and deadlines, and for enduring frozen dinners, and Rachel for designing projects and working long hours to help. And a big thank you to David for helping with photos and other needed tasks.

Our hearts are full of gratitude for all of the artists who contributed original ideas and technical help. Much appreciation to Robert Kirby for his generosity with technical help and expertise on recycled glass. We also acknowledge the wonderful gallery images provided by talented designers for use in this book and the companies that provided materials, tools, and support for the projects.

Thanks to Zachary Williams and Suzy Eaton for the great photos and styling. And thank you to the editors and production staff at Watson-Guptill for the thoughtful care and attention that went into every aspect of creating this book.

CONTENTS

PREFACE

Recycling or reusing materials for crafts or jewelry making has always been an area of interest for many creative types. Recently, the popularity of reuse for crafting has increased significantly due to several factors relating to the times. When the economy is tough, people tend to cut back and spend less, causing them to be more resourceful with the materials they already own. Many feel that consumer consumption creates waste and a drain on the environment. Many "green" movements have sprung up in recent years. Many creative ideas have been spawned from this movement, including jewelry designs.

In times with an uncertain future, there is often also a tendency for people to feel a "nesting" instinct, which draws one to the past and brings back fond memories and feelings of comfort. One might literally use items from the past to craft, giving the new creation a story from earlier times. Or the spirit of the past might be invoked by revisiting former times when resources were scarce and reusing found items was simply a way of life for our ancestors.

Making jewelry from used, discarded, or commonly found objects might sound challenging, and it can be. But anyone who has watched an episode of *Project Runway* knows that the most intriguing designs can be derived from a challenge where the contestants have only a few hours and a pile of candy wrappers to create a runway original. Those designs end up being the memorable ones and are often the most artistic. In writing this book, we discovered that making jewelry from ordinary materials was a lot of fun and very satisfying. To our delight the projects turned out to be very wearable, not to mention inexpensive. Searching for source materials is like a treasure hunt. You have to be careful to *use* the stuff you find rather than get so excited that you decide to hoard every colorful bottle or plastic bag you collect just in case you want to make something later.

The goal in writing this book was to present creative ways to convert ordinary materials that are commonly used or thrown away into beautiful pieces of wearable art jewelry. At first glance a viewer may find it hard to recognize the origins of the material used to make the jewelry, and this adds to the delight and surprise when one realizes that the bracelet that he or she is looking at was once an ordinary plastic bottle. Other source materials used for the jewelry projects might be obvious but designed with a new twist, such as the Silver Spoon Necklace by Jane Salley, where she cut up a spoon into segments to form a vintage-style necklace that is derived from well-known spoon rings or spoon-handle bracelets made from recycled silverware. We didn't necessarily try to disguise the source material when designing the projects, but rather tried to figure out what type of jewelry project would lend itself to be made from the material.

To make jewelry from previously used materials, it helps to look at the material in its basic form. For example, you might ask yourself, "Is it metal, glass, or plastic?" and then treat the material with the appropriate tools and skill set necessary to make something with it. This allows you to look at things differently once you realize that, for example, all metals have common properties and thus riveting a tin can is no different than riveting a sterling silver piece. As is the case with various metals, plastics and fibers share unique properties and can often be treated with the same (or similar) tools and techniques. Mixed media pieces can get a bit trickier because you have to think about ways to combine different materials using the right tools and supplies for optimum success.

The projects in this book use a variety of materials and techniques. Traditional techniques for jewelry making and safety hints are offered throughout to give you the skills needed to create all kinds of great jewelry projects. As for the materials, there is plenty of room for substitution and adaptation if you don't have the exact materials listed for a particular project. The whole idea behind the projects is to use what you have on hand and recycle your own materials—you'll be amazed at how you can make stunning jewelry pieces out of things some might consider trash! It's a great time to be inspired to make jewelry, since no material is off limits and the pressure is off to use precious materials that are cost prohibitive for many aspiring to create.

Sewing notions, like these snaps, can be used in innovative ways to create jewelry.

Ordinary plastic bottles were used to make this bracelet and pins.

1

ESSENTIAL
Tools, Materials, and Techniques

Materials for Upcycling

All of the projects in this book use material that was previously used for another purpose. Metal tins, plastic bottles, broken glass, and even cassette tapes are some of the materials that were recycled into jewelry pieces. Many of the items used to make the jewelry can be found in the home or office and are often things that are typically thrown away. Some of the projects feature collectible items such as silver, china, or miniature toys that can be repurposed to create a piece of jewelry by using mixed media or jewelry-making techniques.

In addition to the found objects used to create the projects, you will need basic tools and supplies such as jewelry-making tools, adhesives, and common craft supplies. These can be found in craft or hardware stores, or ordered from specialty shops online. The resource section at the end of the book will help you in your quest to find the right supplies.

If you have trouble finding just the right material, antique and thrift stores are often a good place to look. Online auction sites are also a good source for finding one person's trash that becomes another's treasure.

Found objects and collectibles are fun to use in jewelry designs. It is a great way to showcase your favorite trinkets or pay tribute to small items that may have sentimental value or a family history.

Jewelry-making Basics

This chapter provides an overview of some basic tools and techniques that are universal for jewelry making—regardless of the type of material being used to make the project. The following chapters are organized according to the type of material used for the projects. Each of these chapters opens with information on the specific tools and techniques that are needed to work with that particular material.

TOOLS

Good-quality jeweler's pliers and wire cutters make a difference in the quality of your work. The basic pliers and cutters needed for the projects in this book are as follows.

CHAIN NOSE PLIERS These are used to open and close jump rings. They are also used to grip or hold wire or to crimp the ends of a wire wrap. These are similar to needle nose pliers, but do not have teeth like needle nose pliers do.

ROUND NOSE PLIERS These are essential for forming wire loops. They have a graduated tip for making loops of various sizes.

WIRE CUTTERS A good pair of side flush cutters will cut the end of a wire cleanly. Use your good pair for fine wirework to make precise close cuts. An old pair of wire cutters or a heavy-duty pair from the hardware store is good to have for heavy gauges of wire or for cutting lengths of wire. Don't cut heavy wire with your good pair or you'll damage them.

JEWELRY FINDINGS

Findings are the components you'll need to assemble the jewelry. The list includes items such as wire, head pins, clasps, and jump rings, just to name a few. There are techniques associated with each finding that are helpful to master. With a little practice, skills such as wire wrapping, riveting, and closing jump rings will serve you well, as these are commonly used in jewelry making.

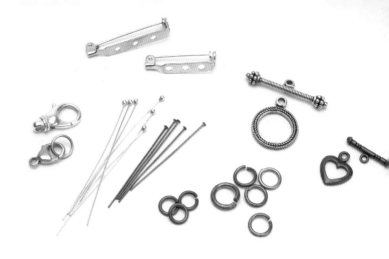

Basic jewelry findings (from far left, clockwise): lobster claw clasps, pin back findings, toggle and bar clasps, jump rings, flat head pins, ball head pins.

HEAD AND EYE PINS A head pin is a short wire with a ball or flat pad on one end. You can thread a bead on a head pin and then form a loop at the top with round nose pliers to make a loop for hanging. An eye pin is similar to a head pin, except it has a loop at the end instead of a ball or flat pad. See the wireworking section following for how to form wire head pins.

JUMP RINGS These are small wire rings that can be purchased or made from wire. If you want to make your own jump rings, see the Sewing Snap Jewelry project on page 133 for directions. Jump rings are used to attach charms and to make jewelry links. The following section on wireworking describes how to use jump rings for jewelry making.

PIN BACKS Pin backs are available in various lengths and metals. The decorative part of the pin can be glued in place or attached mechanically by sewing or riveting to the pin back.

CLASPS Clasps are the closures needed for the ends of a necklace or bracelet. Traditional jewelry clasps include lobster claw, loop-and-toggle, and hook-and-eye styles. The type of closure selected for each project in this book was designed to complement the recycled material used and enhance the aesthetic look of the piece. For example, many fabric or fiber projects use a hook-and-eye closure, which is actually a sewing notion. Buttons and loop closures are also clasp types borrowed from the sewing aisle. Clasps can be purchased or can be custom made to accommodate your design.

EAR WIRES Ear wires are found in bead and jewelry supply stores. As with clasps, choose a metal that matches the style of your design. They are simple to attach with a jump ring, or sometimes they end with a loop that can be opened with pliers to attach to the decorative part of your earring design.

Basic wireworking tools (from left to right): chain nose pliers, wire cutters, needle nose pliers, round nose pliers.

Wireworking Techniques

Wire is used to connect elements together and for decorative purposes. It is available in various metals and thicknesses. Pliers and cutters are the tools you will need when it comes to wirework.

MAKING A WRAPPED WIRE LOOP

Wire wrapping is used to secure wire ends either at the base of a loop or along a section of wire to cover it. Wrapped wire is functional as well as decorative. One of the most basic jewelry-making skills to learn is how to form loops and wraps with wire.

1. Make a 90° bend in the wire.

2. Form a loop with round nose pliers.

3. Hold the loop with chain nose pliers. Wrap the wire around the base of the loop a few times to secure.

4. To connect segments of wrapped loops together, simply add a finished wrapped loop to an open loop before wrapping it. Clip off the excess wire with wire cutters and tuck in the end of the wire in with chain nose pliers.

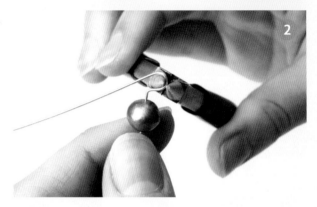

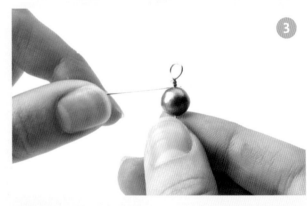

FORMING HEAD AND EYE PINS

To make a bead dangle, use round nose pliers to make a loop at the wire end of a beaded head or eye pin. The loop allows you to attach the head pin dangle to another wire segment or to attach to an ear wire or chain, for example. For extra security, wrap the end of the wire head pin at the base of the formed loop a few times after attaching to the wire or chain. The wire is wrapped in the same manner as it is for making wire-wrapped loops as described on opposite page.

OPENING AND CLOSING JUMP RINGS

Jump rings are rings made of wire that can be opened with pliers to connect jewelry parts. Open and close them as directed below using two pairs of pliers.

Open jump rings with two pair of chain nose pliers in a twisting motion. Pull one of the pliers toward you and push the other pair away from you to open the jump ring, pushing the wire ends out to the sides.

To close the jump ring, bring the wires back to meet in the center from the sides, in the same fashion as they were opened.

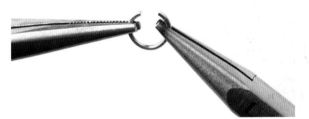

Do not pull open and apart as shown in this photo; this weakens the jump ring and adds stress to the metal.

Tools for Cutting, Piercing, and Punching

Good cutting tools are vital for the success of a project. There are scissors or shears for paper, leather, and even metal. Keep your cutting tools separate and use them only for the material they were intended for to optimize the life of each one.

OLD, INEXPENSIVE SCISSORS These might be your most valuable tool for cutting up materials that might otherwise ruin your good scissors. Old scissors can be used to cut up materials such as plastic bottles, heavy cardboard, or heavy cords.

SEWING SCISSORS These should be used only to cut fabric, thread, and light cord.

LEATHER SHEARS Scissors made specifically for cutting leather are extremely sharp and will cut clean edges through the tough skin.

METAL SHEARS AND TIN SNIPS These are designed for cutting tin and thin gauges of soft metals such as silver or copper—22-gauge is probably the thickest metal you should attempt to cut with good shears to avoid damaging them. Use heavy tin snips from the hardware store to deconstruct tins or cut heavier gauges of metal if needed.

JEWELRY SAW If you feel comfortable using a jewelry saw, you can cut metal and plastic with ease without worrying about the thickness of the material. Just make sure the corresponding blade is appropriate for the material and thickness.

ELECTRIC DRILL For specific cutting and piercing needs, an electric drill or rotary tool, such as a Dremel, has various drilling and cutting attachments that provide the right tool for the task at hand. Cutting disks are available for cutting metal, plastic, and other materials, such as wood. Diamond-coated bit core or blunt-tip bits will drill though china and glass; water is used to lubricate and cool the drill bit as it works its way through the glass.

HAND DRILL AND PIN VISE Use a hand drill or pin vise to drill through plastic, resin, or metal. This type of drill allows you to drill slowly to avoid overheating the plastic, which would stick to the drill bit if it were to be drilled with a high-speed electric drill.

PUNCHES To pierce materials, innovative punch tools are available that save time and effort. Small punches made for piercing metal are sold at jewelry-making suppliers. The rivet piercing/setting tool from Crafted Findings is a dual purpose tool that punches and sets rivet.

Scrapbook suppliers carry punches that will pierce through leather, cardboard and paper. The Crop-A-Dile punch is such a tool, and it was used on many of the projects in this book. The same tool serves to set eyelets after holes are punched, which makes it a great all-purpose essential.

X-ACTO KNIVES These craft knives are handy for cutting through plastic shapes or areas that are difficult to cut with scissors.

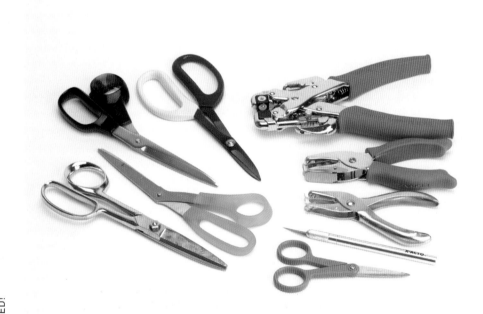

Cutting and punching tools (from lower left): leather shears, inexpensive all-purpose scissors, fabric scissors, tin shears, Crop-A-Dile punch and setter, standard hole punch, mini hole punch, craft knife, small pointed scissors.

Glues and Adhesives

A common challenge facing crafters is deciding which adhesive or glue to use to complete a project. This is especially true when working with unconventional materials such as plastic or leather. The adhesives used in this book fall into three categories: glues for bonding hard surfaces together, adhesives for attaching a hard object to a soft porous surface, and glues for adhering soft pliable porous materials to each other. The detailed information on the various types of adhesives below will help you to figure out which type of adhesive or glue is best to use for any given project.

TWO-PART EPOXY RESIN Hard, nonporous surfaces like glass, plastic, and metal usually require two-part epoxy resin formulations for optimum strength. Epoxy resin glue can be found in hardware or craft stores. It is sold in two-part dispenser tubes. The two parts must be mixed in equal portions to properly catalyze. They set up in minutes or hours, depending on the brand. Sand or roughen up the surfaces to be adhered for best results. Care must be taken to properly measure and mix the epoxy for it to cure with a hard acrylic finish. It is considered permanent, so care should be taken for proper application and cleanup.

JEWELRY GLUES To attach a hard object such as a button to a soft surface like fabric or leather, use a gem or jewelry glue. This type of adhesive is generally a thick formulation of glue that has enough body to hold a gem in place. It is found in fabric and craft stores. The glue is flexible when dry, which helps it to "give" when applied to fibers or leather. Gem-Tac is a favorite product because it holds up well and dries clear. Similar adhesives are found wherever leather supplies are sold. The viscosity of leather adhesive is similar to that of rubber cement, and it is perfect for attaching leather pieces.

WHITE WATER-BASED GLUES These products are good for adhering soft materials to each other. Thick white glue, such as The Ultimate by Crafter's Pick, Sobo, or Aleene's Tacky Glue, is all-purpose craft glue that is thick enough to glue fabric, suede, and felt pieces together. It works well because the glue does not soak or bleed into the fabric, which gives you control and good adhesion. The glue also dries clear. Thinner formulations of white glue such as Mod Podge are good for adhering and sealing materials like paper.

OTHER TYPES OF ADHESIVES A few other types of glues are mentioned in the book for specific projects. Hot melt glue is used for tacking things quickly when time is of the essence for the success of constructing a project such as the T-shirt Rose Jewelry (see page 101). A hem sealant, such as Fray Check, is designed to provide an invisible barrier to prevent fraying of ribbon, cord, or fabric. Clear-drying glues can also be used as a sealants for fabric. For finishing the ends of cords, use jewelry cement such as G-S Hypo Cement, which is available in a fine-tipped tube to provide a tidy finish for delicate cord ends or tight areas where just a tiny dot of glue is required.

Adhesives (from left to right): quick-setting two-part epoxy resin, leather and suede glue, Mod Podge white glue, leather cement, thick white glue, fabric adhesive, jewelry cement.

2

UPCYCLED

METAL AND WIRE

Working with Recycled Metal

Scrap metal comes in many forms. At a time when precious metals can be very costly for jewelry making, the idea of recycled metal is appealing. Vintage tins, old jewelry pieces, silverware, and pieces of scrap metal can all be used with traditional jewelry-making techniques to make mixed media pieces.

Metal requires a few specific jewelry-making tools and techniques, which are the same for working with all types of metal. It's also helpful to know a few simple terms, such as "gauge," which indicates the thickness of the metal or wire. For gauge, the higher the number, the thinner the metal, so, for example, 28-gauge metal or wire will be thinner than 20-gauge. Conversion charts (which can be found online) are helpful for determining what gauge a piece of metal or wire is based on a measurement.

BENCH TOOLS

Metal requires a few specific jewelry-making tools—hammers, riveting tools, punches, and cutting and sanding tools are used universally on all metal projects regardless of the type of metal. Here is a list.

FILES I use large or medium-sized files to quickly file wire ends to make rivets or to file rough edges of various materials, including metals and plastic. I also use small needle files to reach small areas. These come in a set and are shaped differently; which you use depends on what you need to file. Round file shapes are good for holes; flat files are good for squaring off the end of a wire.

HAMMERS AND MALLETS Soft hammers or mallets made of materials like nylon or rubber will shape and flatten without marring surfaces, such as a soft metal with a texture. Steel ball peen hammers are needed to flatten and shape metal rivet heads. Hammers are also used to flatten eyelets.

STEEL BLOCK Use steel when you need strength behind a piece as you hammer. Small portable types are available at jewelry suppliers. I like one that has steel on one side and wood on the other, which makes it a handy dual-purpose tool.

RUBBER BLOCK This substitutes as a bench pin or a support when you need to file or drill through metal. Simply hold the piece against the block as you file, changing the position as needed for support as you work.

BENCH PIN A bench pin is a staple when it comes to jewelry making. It acts as a support for filing and sawing and can be substituted for the rubber block where shown in the project steps.

METAL PUNCHES Specific hole punches are manufactured for punching holes in metal. One type has two ends, providing two hole size options. Choose one that corresponds with the rivet wire or eyelet that you are setting.

Bench tools (from lower left clockwise): small needle files, medium file, steel/wood bench block, rubber block, ball peen hammer, mallet, metal punch, two-hole metal punch, chain nose pliers, small chain nose pliers, round nose pliers, wire cutters.

RIVETING

Riveting is a method of connecting pieces of metal without soldering. It is a common cold connection technique. Rivets can be made from a variety of materials, including small finishing nails, pieces of wire, or metal tubing. The following steps show how to form a traditional rivet using a nail or wire.

1. To rivet two pieces of metal together, or to rivet another material to metal using a wire or nail with a head or ball on one end, stack the metal pieces to determine where the rivets will go. Mark the spots on the top piece with a pen. Use a hand punch or drill if needed to pierce a hole in the top piece for the rivets.

2. Stack the two pieces again and mark the first rivet placement through the hole.

3. Mark and punch a hole in the bottom layer with a punch or drill to match the corresponding hole in the other piece. You will be making one rivet at a time to ensure they match up. Note that the rivet wire should fit tightly in the hole. If you have trouble fitting the wire through the hole in the metal, use a small round needle file to enlarge the hole until the wire passes through snugly.

4. Slide a rivet through the holes in both layers with the ball or flat end of the rivet on top of the stack. Flip the piece over and place on a rubber block or bench pin. Use heavy-duty wire cutters to cut the end of the wire close to the metal surface on the back. The rule of thumb for cutting rivets is to trim the exposed wire so that the height equals one half the width of the diameter of the hole. So if the hole is 2 mm in diameter, then the height of the wire rivet exposed would be 1 mm (it doesn't need to be exact; you can just eyeball it).

5. Use a file to shorten and flatten the end of the wire to finish the rivet.

6. Move the piece to a steel block and use a ball peen riveting hammer to flatten and spread the rivet on the back. Work in a circular fashion on top of the wire as you strike to shape and flatten to form the rivet. The flat head of the hammer will flatten and spread the head, and then the ball end will shape and dome it for a nice finish.

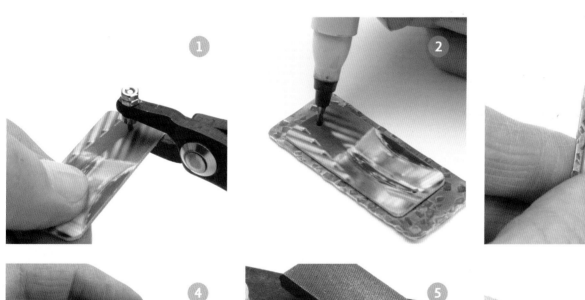

SETTING EYELETS

Eyelet setting is similar to riveting. To set an eyelet, form a hole in the metal or other material that is the same diameter as the eyelet. Place the eyelet in the hole. Check the length of the eyelet and cut if necessary so that the height of the exposed eyelet is one half the diameter of the hole. Flip the piece over so that the open tube is facing up and place on a mat or steel block. Use an eyelet setter placed in the open tube part of the eyelet and hammer the setter to flare. Tap the flared edges with a ball peen hammer around the edges to finish it.

An eyelet can also be set with certain punch tools like the Crop-A-Dile or rivet/piercing setting tool, using hand pressure applied to the jaws of the pliers rather than hammering.

FILING AND SANDING

To file metal, use metal files to smooth and shape edges. Use a rubber block or bench pin to support the piece as you file. File in one direction only, pushing the file away from yourself. Sandpaper will further refine the surface and edges of metal.

ADDING A PATINA

Patina solutions, which are available through jewelry suppliers, add color to or darken the metal through the process of oxidation. They are corrosive in nature, so be sure to follow safety precautions; work in a well-ventilated area and wear gloves and eye protection. Oxidizing chemicals should be kept away from eating areas and disposed of after use. Check with local authorities about proper disposal methods in your area. Liver of sulfur and Black Max are common patina solutions for metal. The following methods describe how to use each chemical.

BLACK MAX Black Max is an oxidizing solution containing hydrochloric acid. It turns silver or copper black. Apply it to the metal with a cotton swab. Rinse and let dry and then buff the raised areas with a polishing pad to remove the patina, leaving it in the recessed areas of the metal.

LIVER OF SULFUR Liver of sulfur is available in solid or liquid form.

1. To begin the patina process using solid chips, dissolve a few chips of dry liver of sulfur in hot water. Heat the metal pieces by running them under hot water first. Use a wire to dip the pieces into the solution and watch as the color moves from golden yellow to blue and finally to blue-black.

2. Remove the pieces from the solution when you like the color. Rinse the metal under cold water and dry the pieces.

3. Polish with fine sandpapers or buffing pads to remove the patina from the raised areas.

Amy DeLeo uses a sterling silver antique spoon and toddler forks to create this bracelet and earrings which she calls The Fork Ran Away with the Spoon. She hand-textured the utensils and added flatback Swarovski crystals to them. Photo by Todd Biss.

Heidi Borchers uses a recycled soda can to create a flower pin.

UPCYCLED METAL AND WIRE

Decorative Tin Jewelry

Designed by Sherri Haab

I am a habitual collector of colorful tins, so this project was a way to justify saving them for a new purpose. Tins are a great source for colorful metal, and I enjoy looking for interesting designs to cut from tins to transform into jewelry. Tins are often given during the holiday season, filled with hot drink mixes, candy, or cookies. Unique old tins can often be found in antique stores. Rust and scratches add to the charm of an old tin, which is perfect for a vintage-style jewelry piece.

Supplies for earrings

- Printed tin *(cookie, coffee, or other type)*
- Tin snips
- Leather gloves
- Fine permanent marker
- Template or pattern for shapes
- Metal shears for cutting tin
- Rubbing alcohol
- Cotton ball
- Flat metal file
- Small round needle file
- 600-grit sandpaper
- Rubber block or bench pin
- Rubber mallet

- 22- or 24-gauge copper shapes or sheet copper to cut shapes *(textured or plain)*
- Handheld 1.25-mm hole punch
- 16-gauge wire copper rivet *(or copper wire to make rivet)*
- Two-hole metal punch or rivet piercing/setting tool *(Crafted Findings)*
- Heavy-duty wire cutters *(inexpensive type from hardware store)*
- Small ball peen hammer
- Steel block *(Volcano Arts)*
- $\frac{1}{16}$-inch *(1.5 mm)* eyelets *(Volcano Arts)*
- Eyelet-setting tool *(mini size for $\frac{1}{16}$ eyelets)*
- Chain nose pliers
- Ear wires

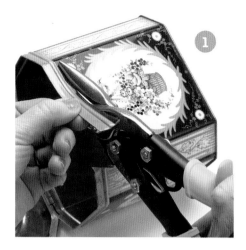

1. Use tin snips to cut through rim and seams to deconstruct the tin. The snips cut through the tough part of the lid. Cut out a panel section with the snips.

2. Use a template or make a pattern to trace around for your metal shape. Choose an illustration printed on the tin to cut the shape from. A fine permanent marker works well to draw the shape. This shape will be stacked and riveted on top of a larger piece of copper.

3. Cut out the tin shape using metal shears.

4. Wipe off the pen lines with a cotton ball and rubbing alcohol.

5. File the edges to smooth and refine. Medium-sized files work for most edges, but you may want to use small files to smooth hard-to-reach areas. Use a rubber block or bench pin if you have one to support the cut shape as you file. Remember to file in one direction only, pushing the file forward. Finish with 600-grit sandpaper to further refine the edges if needed.

6. Flatten the shape with a rubber mallet on a steel block if necessary.

7. The shape will be riveted onto a plain or textured sheet of copper. You can purchase pre-cut shapes from jewelry supply stores or you can cut your own shapes using metal shears or a jewelry saw. If you are using shears, it's best to use a thin gauge of metal, such as 22-gauge or thinner. Sand or file the shape to round corners and to refine if necessary after cutting. Stack the pieces to determine where the rivets will go. Mark the rivet placements on the copper piece with a pen. Use a 1.25-mm hole punch to pierce the metal for the 16-gauge rivets on this piece.

NOTE:
As an extra safety measure, you can wear gloves while you deconstruct the tin using heavy-duty tin snips.

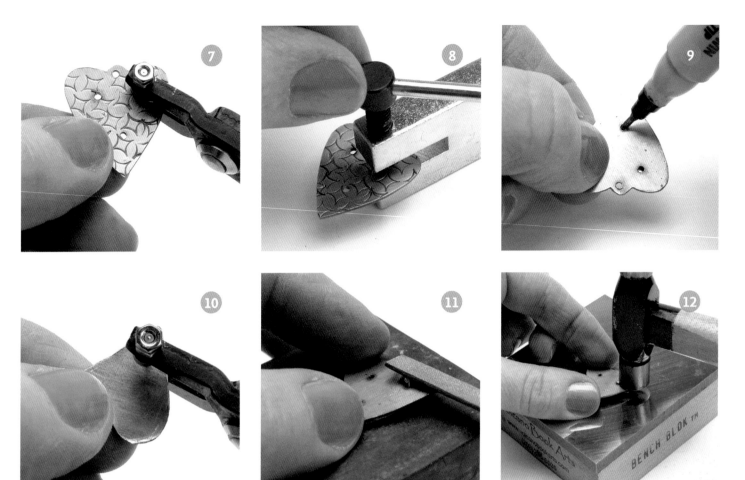

8. Punch a larger hole in the top of the piece to place an eyelet. Use the 1.6-mm side of the two-hole metal punch to accommodate a 1/16-inch metal eyelet or the rivet piercing/setting tool. Both punches screw down through the metal to form a hole, however the rivet piercing/setting tool also sets the rivet without the need for hammering as described in step 15.

9. Stack the two pieces of metal (copper and tin) again and mark one of the rivet placements through the hole.

10. Punch through the tin with the handheld 1.25-mm punch to match the corresponding hole from the other piece. You will be making only one rivet at a time to ensure they match up. Note that rivet wire should fit tightly in the hole. If you have trouble fitting the wire through the hole in the metal, use a small round needle file to enlarge the hole until the wire passes through but still fits snugly.

11. Slide a copper rivet through both layers through the punched holes with the ball or flat end of the rivet on the patterned tin side of the metal stack. Flip the piece over and place onto a rubber block or bench pin. Use heavy-duty wire cutters to cut the end of the wire close to the metal surface on the back. The rule of thumb for cutting rivets is to trim the exposed wire so that the height equals one half the width of the diameter of the hole. So if the hole is 1.25 mm in diameter, then the height of the wire rivet exposed would be 0.6 mm (it doesn't need to be exact; you can just eyeball it). Use a file to shorten and flatten the end of the wire.

12. Move the piece to a steel block and use a ball peen riveting hammer to flatten and spread the rivet on the back. Work in a circular fashion on top of the wire as you strike to shape and flatten to form the rivet. Use the flat head of the hammer to flatten and spread the head, and then use the ball end to shape and dome it for a nice finish.

13. To form the next rivet, punch through the next hole and form the rivet as directed in steps 10–12. Form as many rivets as needed to accommodate your design.

14. Place the eyelet in the hole at the top of the piece. If the hole is too small, use a round needle file to expand it until the eyelet fits.

15. Position the piece on the steel block over the edge to clear the rivets. Use an eyelet-setting tool and a hammer to softly hammer and flare the eyelet. Remove the setter and tap the edges with a ball peen hammer until the eyelet is tight with the metal. If you hammer too long or too aggressively it will continue to spread and flatten the eyelet, which may close the hole. You may want to practice with placing a few eyelets on scrap metal first to get a feel for setting them. (If you used the rivet piercing/setting tool to make the hole you can skip this step and use the eyelet side of the tool instead.)

16. Use chain nose pliers to attach the ear wires.

MAKING YOUR OWN RIVETS
To make your own rivets using 16-gauge wire: Place the end of the wire in a vise, or clamp in the side of heavy-duty needle nose pliers. The pliers can make a makeshift vise if you are in a hurry. Leave just enough wire exposed to form one end of the rivet (approximately 0.6 mm). With the wire firmly held in place with pliers or vise, hammer the end of the wire with a ball peen hammer to spread the end of the wire and form the rivet head.

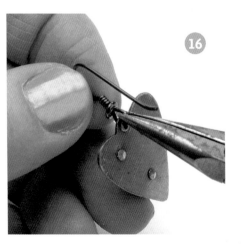

Variation: TIN PENDANT

This pendant can be made by basically following the same steps for the earrings with the addition of the few steps below. The background copper piece for this pendant was etched and then patina was added to darken the recessed areas of the pattern. The tin was cut into an oval shape and layered onto the cut background shape.

Additional Supplies
- Two ⅛-inch metal eyelets (*Volcano Arts*)
- Eyelet-setting tool for ⅛-inch eyelets
- Jump ring
- Chain with clasp
- Beads
- Eye pin
- Head pin

1. Punch a large hole into the copper background shape for an ⅛-inch eyelet for hanging the pendant and another in the bottom if desired for a bead dangle. I used the large punch side of the two-hole metal punch (2.3 mm) to make the initial hole for the eyelet and then used a round needle file to enlarge the hole until the eyelet fit (about 3 mm). You can also drill a hole that is the right size to begin with.

2. Set an eyelet for hanging. Add an additional eyelet at the bottom if another hole was made at the bottom to hang a bead dangle.

3. Add a jump ring to attach the pendant to chain.

4. Form the bead dangle using an eye and head pin each threaded with beads. Form wire-wrapped loops to attach the beaded eye pin and then head pin at the base. Clip off the ends of the wires with wire cutters.

Silver Spoon Necklace

Designed by Jane Salley

Jane mixes the old with the new to create unique jewelry. Her pieces project a soft feminine feel with floral patterns and jewels. For this necklace, she found a clever way to use a beautiful silver spoon for an elegant beaded necklace design. To make a silver spoon necklace, look for solid sterling silver instead of silver-plated cutlery. Plated silver is composed of a base metal that is extremely hard to cut through. Old silver can be found in thrift or antique stores. Jane used a real dried rose as the center focal piece in this design. In describing her necklace, she remarks: "When I saw the big silver spoon I wondered about all the family dinners it had served. I wanted to honor this humble object that had lost its place in the world by giving it a new purpose."

Supplies

- Sterling silver spoon
- Jeweler's saw or Dremel with cutoff wheel *(rotary disk specifically for cutting metal)*
- Eye protection
- Vise
- Permanent marker
- Bench pin or rubber block
- Metal file
- Sandpaper
- 3M polishing papers to smooth cut metal *(six grits)*
- Drill press or flex shaft tool
- 1.3-mm drill bit *(for making holes in spoon)*

- Half-hard 24-gauge sterling silver round wire
- Beads and pearls
- Jump rings
- Clasp finding
- Dried rosebud
- Quick-setting epoxy resin
- Wax paper and toothpick for mixing resin
- Rivet or escutcheon pins *(small brass nail from hardware store)*
- Round nose pliers
- Chain nose pliers
- Wire cutters

1. Use a jeweler's saw or Dremel fitted with a cutoff wheel for metal to remove the bowl of the spoon from the handle, leaving a stub where the chain will attach. Be sure to wear eye protection while cutting. It is also handy to hold the spoon in a vise to keep it secure for extra control while cutting.

2. Cut the handle into segments (use a permanent marker to mark the cuts before cutting).

3. Smooth the rough edges by filing them on a bench pin or rubber block. Sand the edges with six grits of fine polishing papers, working progressively finer for a smooth finish to the metal.

4. Use a flex shaft tool or drill press at a slow speed to drill through the metal. Drill holes in the spoon handle segments to accommodate jump rings. Drill a hole at the top of the bowl for attaching the beaded necklace. Drill a hole in the center of the bowl of the spoon for a rivet or pin that will secure the rosebud. Use the 24-gauge sterling silver wire to make wire-wrapped loops with the beads and pearls (see page 14 for more about wire-wrapping techniques). Link the beads and handle segments together with jump rings to create a design for both sides of the necklace.

5. Attach the bowl of the spoon to the necklace sides using large sturdy jump rings to connect the pieces. Attach a clasp to the other ends.

6. Roughen the rivet or pin that the rose will attach to with sandpaper or a file so that the epoxy will grab when the rosebud is attached. Clip off the end of the wire if it is too long. Drill or pierce the base of the rosebud. Mix the quick-setting epoxy resin on the wax paper with a toothpick, according to the manufacturer's instructions. Fill the hole with epoxy.

7. Inset the rivet or pin through the back of the spoon bowl and then attach the rosebud, fixing it in place. Let the epoxy harden.

Beaded Telephone Wire Bracelet

Designed by Michelle Haab

Michelle found an interesting way to reuse materials that were lying around the house. In describing her inspiration, she says, "I grew up in a family of engineers, and so scraps from electronic parts and plastic-coated wires were always around and provided fascinating craft material. My grandfather worked for the local phone company, so telephone wire was a natural choice for a retro-style bracelet complete with a vintage toy engineer or nostalgic button attached to complete a piece derived from past memories."

Telephone wire is sometimes hard to come by, but if you can get a small bundle of scrap wire from your local phone company you will have plenty of wire to make projects with. The wire is coated with colored plastic, and it is very easy to wrap and form designs with it. If you can't get telephone wire you can use the same techniques using other types of recycled wire.

Supplies
- Plastic-coated telephone wire
- Wire cutters
- Button with loop or shank or small plastic toy
- Pin vise with small drill bit *(if toy needs a loop attachment)*
- Metal wire to make loop *(if toy needs a loop attachment)*
- Two-part quick-setting epoxy resin *(if toy needs a loop attachment)*
- Chain nose pliers
- Round nose pliers
- Clasp

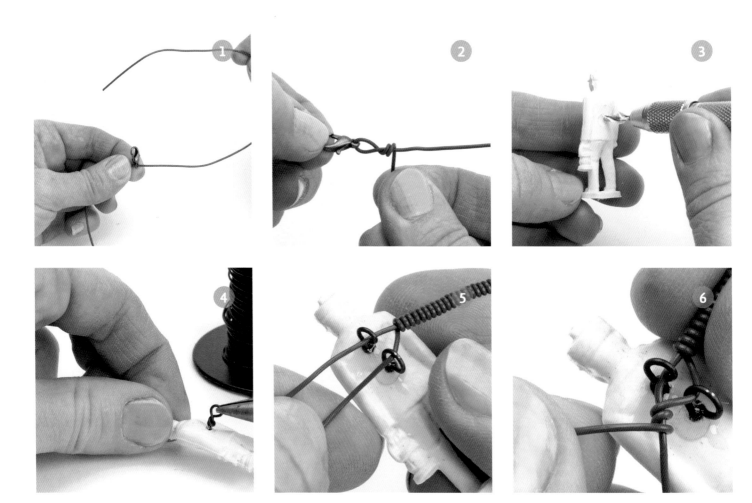

1. Cut 3 feet of wire for the bracelet using wire cutters. Measure the size you would like the finished bracelet to be and add 3 inches. Slide a clasp onto the wire to this point and make a loop with the round nose pliers by wrapping the longer end of the wire around the shorter length. The shorter end of the wire will be the "core" of the bracelet that the longer wire is wrapped around to form the design.

2. Wrap tight, neat coils around the shorter core wire until you reach the middle of the bracelet.

3. If you're using a toy that doesn't have an existing shank or loop, you can make your own loop to affix to the back of a charm. To make a wire loop or shank to attach to the back of a plastic piece, use a hand drill (pin vise) to drill holes partway through the back of the piece. Here two holes were drilled for two wire loops.

4. Make small wire loops with round nose pliers and twist. Clip off the end with wire cutters and use two-part quick-setting epoxy resin to glue the loops in place onto the back of the piece. Let the epoxy set as directed.

5. Thread the button or toy charm onto the core wire, or if you have two loops thread both wires through the loops (as shown in this photo).

6. Continue to wrap the long wire over the core wire to secure the piece to the bracelet. Keep wrapping until the bracelet is close to the finished length.

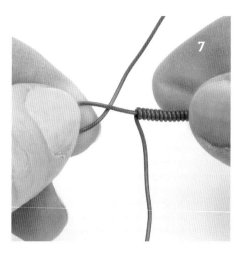

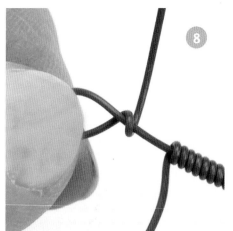

7. Measure the bracelet to fit and then make a loop on the end of the short core wire with the round nose pliers.

8. Wrap the end of the wire a few times under the loop until the wrapped wires meet.

9. Clip off the excess wire.

10. Use chain nose pliers to tuck the wires in neatly to finish. You can add pieces such as an old pin attached to a multiple strand design or add beads for a different look.

UPCYCLED METAL GALLERY

1. *Brush Ring* by Susan Lenart Kazmer. Photo by Mavis Dean.

2. *Soda Can Heart Pin* by Heidi Borchers. Recycled aluminum. Photo by the artist.

3. *Mixed Media Pendant with Metal Ruler* by Susan Lenart Kazmer. Photo by Mavis Dean.

4. *Mixed Media Pendant with Antique Key and Resin-filled Bezel with Paper* by Susan Lenart Kazmer. Photo by Mavis Dean.

3

UPCYCLED
PLASTIC

Working with Recycled Plastics

The use of plastics for jewelry making became very popular in the 1920s and 1930s with the development of plastic materials such as celluloid and Bakelite. Improvements in both types of plastics combined with shortages of other materials during wartime led to a demand for plastic adornment, which inspired quite a few jewelry trends.

In recent years, discarded plastic surrounds us in abundance—plastic bags, bottles, and containers seem to be everywhere. Plastic is one of the most common materials in desperate need of recycling. Modern jewelry designers are now recycling not only all kinds of discarded plastic but also actual vintage jewelry pieces made of plastic into new designs. Resin, Plexiglas, PVC, and even recycled food containers are finding their way into art galleries and jewelry displays. Plastic varies in chemical makeup, ranges from transparent to opaque, and is available in a rainbow of colors. Even though plastics differ, they share common properties and can be manipulated with tools, heat, drilling, and sanding. Imitative techniques and combining plastic with other media make it a fascinating material to use in jewelry design.

Rebecca Crawford uses recycled plastic to make her Polka Dot Necklace. *Photo by the artist.*

CUTTING

To cut plastic, use a craft knife or old scissors, as cutting plastic will dull good tools. A simple cut plastic shape hung from a jump ring can make a very strong statement in a jewelry design.

DRILLING AND SANDING

Plastic can be sanded or drilled. If you drill or sand plastic, always do so by hand, which produces better results than using a high-speed electrical method. Use a hand drill, which will drill smoothly through the plastic without melting on the drill bit. As you sand, do so with wet/dry sandpaper under water to keep the dust down. It is dangerous to breathe dust from many materials, including plastic. The water also helps to keep the plastic from redepositing itself into the material. To sand plastic, start with grits such as 320 or 400 and move progressively higher through 600, 800, and 1000 grits on up if more refinement is required.

HEATING

When plastics are heated they will melt and thicken. All plastics respond differently to heat, so great care should be taken for safety when heating plastics.

SAFETY CONSIDERATIONS

It is important to consider safety when it comes to plastics. Plastics can release toxic fumes, especially when melted, so ventilation and respiratory protection are very important. A ventilator mask with filters rated for fumes should be worn. Although plastics may look alike, they may produce entirely different results if the wrong type is used for a project. Heating with relatively low heat for brief periods of time and with proper ventilation is key when working with plastic.

Beth Todd uses ordinary plastic bags to make her Crocheted Plastic Bracelet *(for another view of this piece see page 75). Photo by the artist.*

Crocheted Plastic Bracelet *(for another view of this piece see page 75).

Gift Card Jewelry

Designed by Richard Salley

Richard found himself inspired to make jewelry out of colorful decorative gift cards. He comments, "As a frequent Starbucks customer I began to collect their gift cards because I loved the interesting images on the cards. I then decided to incorporate parts of the cards into jewelry pieces rather than throw them away." Richard combines plastic with metal to make mixed media earrings by riveting the two materials together. You can use other cards such as old credit cards for a similar look.

Supplies for earrings

- Plastic gift card
- Permanent marker
- Scissors
- 24-gauge copper sheet metal or purchased metal shapes
- Jeweler's saw *(for cutting your own shapes)*
- Saw blade size 4/0 or 5/0 *(for cutting your own shapes)*
- Texturing hammer
- Steel block
- Rubber block or bench pin
- Metal file

- Patina solution
- Polishing pad for removing patina
- 1.25-mm metal punch or #56 drill bit and drill
- 18-gauge brass escutcheon pins *(small brass nails, from hardware store)*
- Heavy-duty wire cutters to cut pins
- Safety glasses
- Hammer for riveting
- Chain nose pliers
- Ear wires

1. Draw or trace the shapes you want onto the gift card with a permanent marker, then cut them out with scissors. These will be riveted onto the metal background shapes in the next step. Cut 24-gauge sheet metal slightly larger than the card pieces to create the background pieces using a jeweler's saw, or use purchased metal shapes. Texture and patina the metal or leave plain. Textures can be created using a texturing hammer on a steel block.

2. Use a metal file on a rubber block or bench pin to round corners.

3. Patina the metal with an oxidizing solution, wiping off the high spots of texture with a polishing pad.

4. Punch or drill holes near the top or bottom of the gift card. Use a 1.25-mm punch or a #56 drill bit. These will accommodate the 18-gauge rivets (escutcheon pins) you will use.

5. Position the gift card over the sheet metal piece and mark one hole.

6. Punch or drill one hole using the same size punch that was used in step 4.

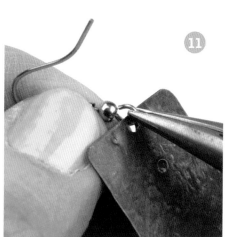

7. Prepare to rivet the gift card to the sheet metal using an 18-gauge brass escutcheon pin. These can be found at most hardware stores and are used as decorative nails for small ornamental pieces. Push the pin through the card and metal.

8. Clip off the back of the pin so that it is short enough to form the rivet. See page 21 for how to cut wire prior to riveting. Be sure to wear eye protection and cover the wire with your hand to catch the cut point of the wire.

9. File the cut wire to flatten the surface prior to riveting.

10. Rivet the wire using the hammer on a steel block. Refer to page 21 for more information on riveting. Punch or drill a second hole in the sheet metal and plastic to make the next rivet. Rivet the card in place.

11. Punch or drill a hole in the sheet metal about $1/16$ inch from the top and attach an ear wire with chain nose pliers to finish the earring.

Variation: HEART PENDANT

Designed by Michelle Haab

This is a variation of the gift card idea that uses credit cards. Michelle chose to use credit and ID cards because they represent something more personal than a gift card. Michelle used portions of the cards featuring her embossed name to personalize the jewelry. Eyelets are used to attach the card pieces to the metal instead of rivets. Be sure to use only parts of the card that won't reveal sensitive information. This project is especially quick and easy as it takes advantage of using a die-cut heart-shaped metal blank and purchased eyelets.

Supplies

- Credit card
- Scissors
- Purchased copper heart shape
- Permanent marker
- Two-hole metal punch (*1.6 and 2.3 mm size*)
- ¹⁄₁₆-inch (*1.5-mm*) eyelets (*Volcano Arts*)
- Eyelet-setting tool (*mini size for ¹⁄₁₆-inch eyelets*)
- Steel block
- Hammer
- Small ball peen hammer
- Chain nose pliers
- Jump ring small enough to fit through eyelet
- Chain for necklace

1. Cut up the card into shapes to fit onto background metal heart piece. Place the first piece onto the background shape and use a marker to mark the eyelet placement. Punch a hole in the plastic card with the 1.6-mm side of the two-hole punch for the first eyelet. Place the card over the heart and mark the hole on the metal. Punch a hole in the metal using the same punch. Set the eyelet in place.

2. Use an eyelet-setting tool, steel block, and a hammer to set the eyelet on the back of the piece. Remove the setter and use a smaller hammer to flatten the eyelet a little more. Punch the next hole through both card and metal layers. Set the next eyelet and then each one after until the piece is secure and you like the design. Use chain nose pliers to attach a jump ring through one of the holes. Attach the finished piece to hang from a purchased chain.

Plastic Bottle Jewelry

Designed by Michelle Haab

Common plastic bottles are a great choice for recycling into jewelry. An enormous number of these bottles are thrown away, so why not see what you can make with them? Some are clear and some are tinted with color. When they are cut into shapes the plastic has a glass-like quality. You can use different parts of the bottle for jewelry. Michelle used the sides and bottom of one bottle to make two different projects.

The bottle we used in this project was a specific type known as PET plastic. PET stands for polyethylene terephthalate, the technical name for a common plastic used as a container for soda pop and water. These types of bottles are labeled with the number 1 inside the arrows on the recycling symbol. Always make sure the bottle you intend to use has this type of marked label to ensure you are using the right type of plastic. Some plastics look similar but do not have the same properties and will not work for the project.

Supplies

- Scissors
- Flower-shaped cookie cutters or handmade flower template
- Clean soda pop or water bottles (*must be PET plastic*)
- Permanent marker
- Paper hole punch (*⅛-inch hole*)
- Respirator fitted with fume filters
- Embossing heat tool
- Ceramic tile
- Wooden dapping punch or other round form
- Soft Flex beading wire (*0.014 fine*)
- FireLine braided bead thread (*6-lb weight*)
- Seed beads size 10/0, crystal clear in color
- Four crimp beads
- Pearls, glass crystal, and small seed beads for flower centers
- Button with a shank to use for a clasp
- Chain nose pliers
- Wire cutters

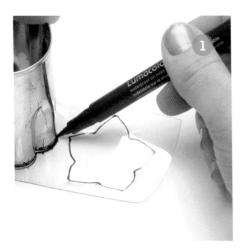 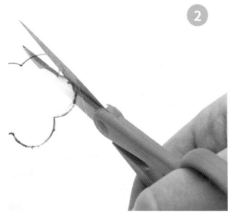  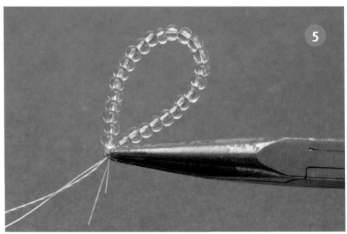

1. Use scissors to cut and remove the bottom section of the bottle (this can be used later to make a flower pin). Cut a panel from the smooth side to work with. Flatten the panel and trace around flower-shaped cookie cutters using a permanent marker to make the flower designs. You can also make your own flower templates if you don't have cookie cutters to use.

2. Cut out the flowers just inside the traced line to avoid the pen marks.

3. Punch a hole in the center of each flower.

4. Prepare for heating the plastic by wearing a respirator to protect you from plastic fumes and choosing a well-ventilated work area. Make sure the respirator is rated for vapors and not just dust. With the flower shape on a tile or other heat-resistant surface, center the wooden dapping punch and press lightly to hold the shape in place. Use the embossing heat tool to evenly heat the plastic and rotate slowly to ensure proper forming. (Wait for the piece to cool before handling.) As the plastic is heated it will shrink and thicken as it curls up to form the shape. The petals won't always be perfect, but this adds character. Make a number of flowers in various shapes to complete the bracelet.

5. To make the bracelet cut one piece of FireLine bead thread and one of Soft Flex beading wire, each about 24 inches in length. Hold them together and thread enough seed beads over both the wire and the thread at one end so that when the row of beads is formed into a loop it fits over the button you will use as the clasp. Slide two crimp beads over both ends to secure the loop, leaving just a small tail of the wire and thread exposed. Use chain nose pliers to flatten and secure the crimps.

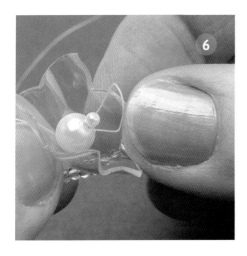

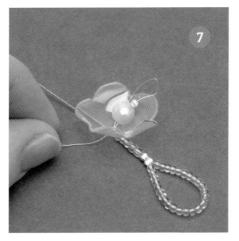

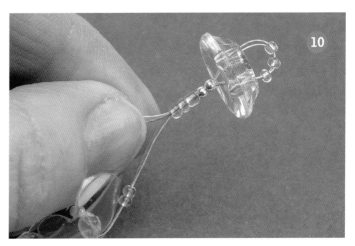

6. Slide a few seed beads over the ends of the exposed wire and thread to hide them. There will be a wire and a thread to work with as you bead. The seed beads will be threaded over both the wire and the thread at the same time. The plastic flowers and crystal and pearls will be threaded onto the thread only. After threading a few more seed beads onto the wire and thread, use the fine thread to add your first flower. Thread up through the flower, through a pearl, through a small seed bead and then back down through the pearl and flower. The small seed bead anchors the pearl to hold it in place.

7. Pull the thread close to the wire cable to pull up the slack.

8. Add beads over both the wire and the thread until you are ready for the placement of the next flower. Repeat steps 6–8 and this step to continue adding flowers along the bracelet. Alternate adding pearls and crystals of various sizes to the centers of the flowers for variety.

9. Add enough seed beads between each flower to avoid crowding and allow the flowers to fit along the line.

10. Once the bracelet is the long enough to fit, string two crimp beads onto both the thread and the wire, then add a two-holed button for the clasp. Bring both the wire and thread up through one of the button holes and add a few seed beads (they will sit on top of the button), and then bring the wire and the thread back through the button and then through the crimp beads along with a few seed beads on the bracelet to hide the ends. Pull secure and flatten the crimps with chain nose pliers to hold. Clip off the excess wire and thread with wire cutters.

Variation: PET BOTTLE PIN

Have you ever noticed that the bottom of most plastic bottles looks just like a molded flower shape? All you need to do is cut it out and you have an instant shape to use for a jewelry design. By melting it slightly you can soften the edges of the cut plastic. Add beads for extra sparkle to make a brooch or pin.

Additional Supplies
- Pin back finding
- Quick-setting epoxy resin
- Wax paper
- Toothpick

1. Use scissors to remove the bottom portion of the soda pop or water bottle. Notice how the cut shape looks like a flower.

2. Trim the edges as shown to shape the edges of the petals.

3. Prepare for heating the plastic by wearing a respirator to protect you from plastic fumes and choosing a well-ventilated work area. Make sure the respirator is rated for vapors and not just dust. With the flower shape on a tile or other heat-resistant surface, center the wooden dapping punch and press lightly to hold the shape in place. Using the embossing heat tool, evenly heat the plastic and rotate around the shape slowly to ensure proper heating. (Wait for the piece to cool before handling.) The piece will shrink slightly and the plastic will thicken.

4. Work on a folded piece of wax paper and mix a small amount of clear quick-setting epoxy resin with a toothpick (see page 17).

5. Use a toothpick to apply the epoxy to set the beads in the center of the flower. Let the piece sit overnight before applying the pin back finding.

6. Once the epoxy has hardened, flip the piece over and apply epoxy to attach the pin back finding.

Crocheted Plastic Bag Bracelet

Designed by Michelle Haab

Almost everyone has plastic shopping bags lying around in various sizes and colors, and usually many more plastic bags than they know what to do with, so here is a great way to use them. Simply cut them up into strips of plastic that can be used for fiber techniques such as weaving or crochet. There is now even a term for this plastic yarn: "plarn." Mix the plastic with other materials such as fiber or yarn scraps. The texture of the plastic in contrast with the yarn adds interest. Yarn also helps to stabilize the crocheted shapes when the two are mixed and can add colors that you might not be able to find in plastic. A guide at the end of the project illustrates how to do basic crochet stitches, and any of these stitches will work with the plastic bag strips. Even if you have never crocheted before, with the help of the guide you will be able to do the basic stitches needed for this project.

Supplies

- Plastic shopping bags in various colors
- Yarn to coordinate with bag colors
- Scissors
- Crochet hook
- Hook-and-eye closure or snaps
- Clear nylon thread
- Sewing needle

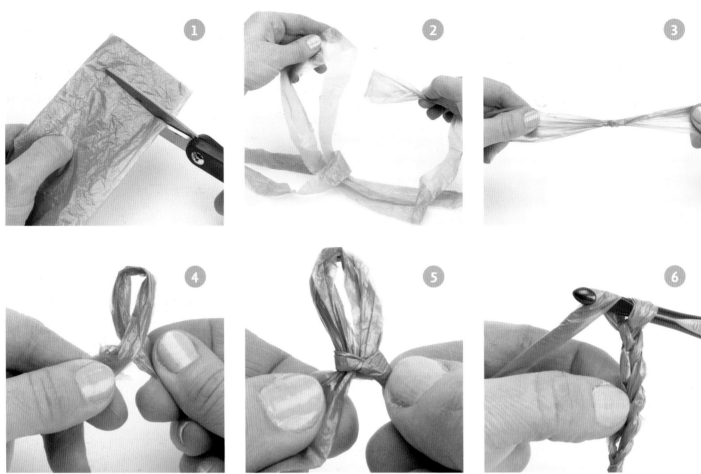

1. Cut strips from colorful plastic bags to crochet with. To cut the strips, fold a plastic bag lengthwise several times to make cutting the strips easier. Cut 1-inch sections across the folded bag to make plastic bag strips (they will be loops).

2. To connect the strips, place the loop of one plastic strip through a new one and then bring the other end of the first back through itself.

3. Pull the strips taut to secure the attachment. Attach a few more strips at this point, or add them as needed as you work to create a length of two-ply plarn. As you work, you'll use both strands together as if they were one.

4. Begin the crochet circle pattern by making a slip knot. A slip knot is started by forming a loop (see the sidebar on page 62 for all the stitches you need for this project).

5. To complete the slip knot, hook the long end of the strip through the loop to form a new loop or completed slip knot. Insert the crochet hook into the slip knot and pull until taut on the hook.

6. Begin with six chain stitches. The strip goes over the hook ("yarn over") and then the loop on the hook is pulled through the slip knot. Continue to pull each loop through the previous one to make a chain of six stitches.

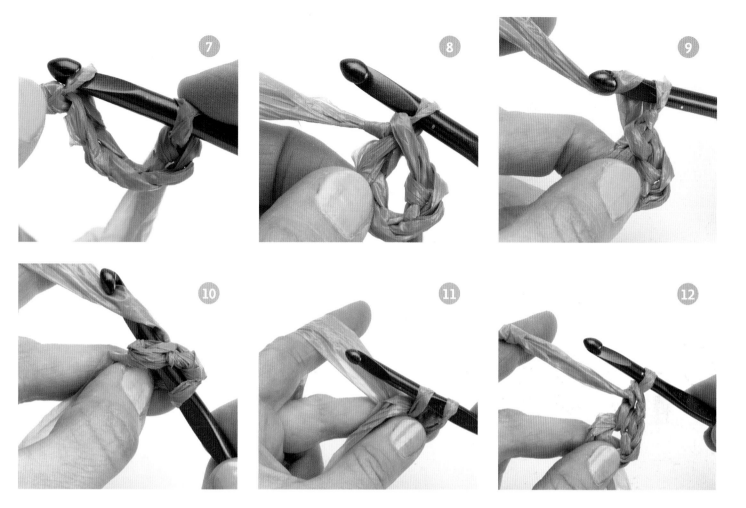

7. Slip the hook into the first stitch to form a ring.

8. Hook the strip through to connect.

9. Chain one stitch.

10. Form single crochet stitches around the ring by placing the hook into the open center of the ring and then yarn over the hook, bringing the strip back through the center.

11. Now you have two loops on the hook.

12. Yarn over and pull through both loops to complete the stitch.

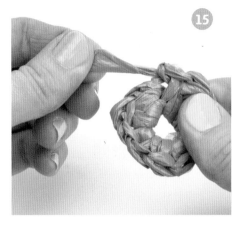

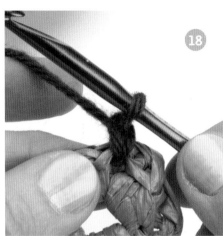

13. Keep making stitches around the ring by inserting the hook in the center to begin each until you cover the ring and reach the first stitch on the round.

14. Finish the round by hooking into top of the first stitch.

15. Yarn over and pull the end of the strip through to make a slip stitch to finish. Cut the end of the strip off and switch to a different color of plastic or use yarn for the next round.

16. To begin the next round, make a slip knot with the yarn.

17. Use the hook to pull the slip knot through one of the stitches on the round. Yarn over and hook through the slip knot to attach.

18. Make another chain stitch.

19. Insert the hook into the next stitch and form a single crochet stitch.

20. Make a single chain stitch between each single crochet stitch.

21. Insert the hook into the next stitch and continue around until you complete the round. Hook into the last stitch, form a slip stitch to finish. Weave the ends of the plastic and yarn into the work to hide.

22. Make a series of round pieces combining yarn and plastic in various sizes for the bracelet. Stitch them together with clear nylon thread to form a pleasing design for the bracelet.

23. Finish the bracelet by sewing on a hook-and-eye closure, or you can substitute snaps if you desire.

Basic Crochet Stitches

Here are a few very basic crochet stitches you'll need to know to make the Crocheted Plastic Bag Bracelet. Even if you have never crocheted before, with a little practice you'll be doing these stitches in no time. One term that is useful to know before you start practicing the stitches is "slip knot," which is a knot that is often used when you attach the yarn to the hook before you begin stitching.

CHAIN STITCH

Place a slip knot on your crochet hook. Yarn over the hook and pull it through the slip knot to form a new loop on the hook. This is the first chain stitch. Repeat to form as many chain stitches as needed.

SLIP STITCH

Insert the hook into the indicated stitch, yarn over the hook, and draw the yarn through both the stitch and the loop on the hook. The slip stitch is often used to finish off the work—when you make the last stitch, clip the yarn, pull the yarn tight, and weave the end of the yarn in to hide it.

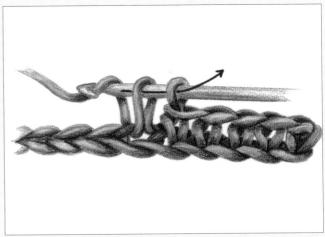

JOINING A RING

A slip stitch can be used to form a ring of stitches. To make a ring, first make a foundation chain as specified in the pattern instructions, and then work a slip stitch into the first chain to join the ring, as shown.

SINGLE CROCHET STITCH

Insert the crochet hook into the indicted stitch, yarn over the hook, and pull the yarn through the stitch to form a loop on the hook; there are now two loops on your hook. Yarn over the hook and draw the yarn through both loops on the hook, as shown.

Illustrations by Laura Polley

Shampoo Bottle Bead Charm Bracelet

Designed by Michelle Haab

Shampoo and soap bottles come in a variety of pretty colors that can easily be cut to make geometric shapes for jewelry charms. Michelle admits: "sometimes I buy certain brands just because I adore the bottle design and color." Here she uses one simple shape and repetition to create this fun tropical-colored bracelet.

Supplies

- Empty shampoo or soap bottles in various opaque colors
- Scissors *(old pair that you don't mind cutting plastic with)*
- Small hole punch
- Wet/dry sandpaper *(400 grit)* or nail file *(600, 800, and 1200 grit if more refining is desired)*
- Gold-colored chain for bracelet
- Gold-colored wire *(28 or 26 gauge)*
- Gold-colored beads
- Gold-colored head pins
- Jump rings
- Clasp
- Fine permanent marker
- Chain nose pliers
- Round nose pliers
- Wire cutters

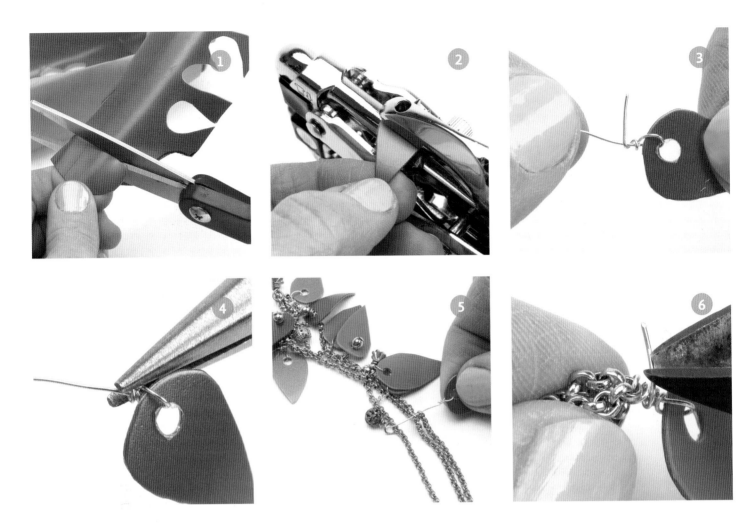

1. Wash and dry empty bottles. Use scissors to cut teardrop shapes from the plastic. Take care not to make unwanted cuts around the shape. If you want shapes to be perfectly uniform, you can draw them with a fine permanent marker first using a stencil or pattern. Cut inside the lines to avoid marks. If you have rough cuts or unwanted marks, sand the edges, working under water with a nail file or 400-grit wet/dry sandpaper to smooth rough edges. You can work progressively finer with 600-, 800-, and 1200-grit sandpaper if more refining is desired.

2. Use a hole punch to pierce a hole in the top of the charm for hanging.

3. Use an existing bracelet or make one with two or three strands of chain. Add a clasp to the ends with jump rings. To attach the charms, loop a piece of wire through the charm. Wrap the wire a few times at the base of the loop to secure the charm.

4. Tuck the end of the wire close to the wrap with chain nose pliers.

5. To attach the charm to the chain, loop the end of the wire attached to the charm through a link along the chain.

6. Wrap the wire at the base of the loop and clip off the excess wire. Keep adding charms along the bracelet to make the design as full as you would like. Add gold-colored beads for decorative accents along the strands using head pins. Make a wrapped loop (see page 14) to attach each bead along the chain.

Bubble Wrap Necklace

Designed by Steven James

Steven is an enthusiastic artist and teacher who uses a variety of recycled materials in his work. On his choice to use bubble wrap for this project, he comments: "I've always been fascinated with the idea of manipulating materials and the science behind creativity. The process of fusing the bubble wrap takes it from one material to something incredibly different, while just slightly retaining some of its original form." This necklace makes the most of bubble wrap's close resemblance to mother-of-pearl. By simply cutting circles of bubble wrap one achieves an elegant yet sophisticated design.

The technique of heat fusing layers of plastic used in this project is versatile and can be used with a variety of plastic materials (including various colors of bubble wrap and plastic shopping bags) to create projects. Creative designs ranging from bracelets to earrings are possible using pieces of fused plastic.

Supplies
- Bubble wrap (*small bubble type; five to seven strips, approximately 8–9 inches long and 2 inches wide*)
- Scissors
- Iron
- Parchment paper
- Circle template
- Pen
- Small hole punch
- Chain nose pliers
- Jump rings
- Small piece of chain (*about 3 inches long*)
- Chain segments for necklace
- Pearls
- 28-gauge wire for each wire-wrapped pearl segment
- Clasp

1. Use the scissors to cut the strips of bubble wrap and release the trapped air by snipping individual bubbles, or leave bubbles intact. Turn on the iron to the wool/no steam setting. Layer two sheets of bubble wrap.

2. Place the two pieces of wrap inside a piece of parchment paper and fold to close.

3. Iron the entire surface, front and back, for approximately 30 seconds.

4. Allow to cool, then repeat the process, layering additional pieces of bubble wrap on top of one another. Continue until you reached the desired thickness, usually 5–7 pieces.

JEWELRY UPCYCLED!

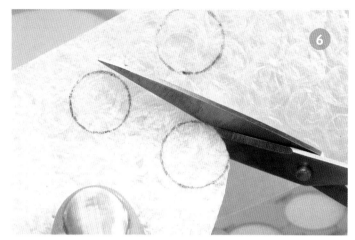

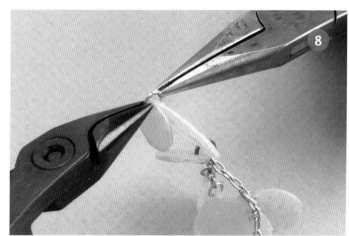

5. Allow the plastic to cool before cutting the circles. Use a circle template with a pen to mark small circles of various sizes onto the plastic. Make about 10–15 in a range of sizes These will be attached in a cluster to form the focal design of the necklace.

6. Cut out each circle with sharp pointed scissors.

7. Punch a small hole at the top of each circle.

8. Use chain nose pliers to attach some circles along a small piece of chain using jump rings. Punch holes in the bottom of a few of these circles to link smaller circles to them with jump rings for added dimension and fullness. The design will resemble a cluster of grapes with fullness at the top, tapering off with smaller circles at the bottom of the chain. To form the necklace, make wire-wrapped segments using 28-gauge wire and pearls. Before wrapping at the end of each pearl, add a chain segment to each side to form the length of the necklace. When your desired length is achieved, attach a clasp and then attach the bubble cluster to the necklace using chain nose pliers and jump rings.

Braided Cassette Tape Bracelet

Designed by Michelle Haab

Michelle was excited to find a way to reuse old cassette tapes and transform them into new bracelets. After various attempts to use fiber techniques with the tape, she selected a kumihimo wheel as the best way for braiding the tape into a pattern. The braided pattern creates faceted angles along the tape that reflect light to add sparkle. The wheel adds some control as you work with the stretchy tape. If you use even tension as you weave, you will see a beautiful braided pattern emerge. Make a bunch to wear in a layered stack or add beads along the way for color. No one will ever guess what they are made of.

Supplies
- Cassette tape
- Weave Wheel for kumihimo *(Toner Crafts)*
- Scissors
- Binder clip
- Large-holed beads
- Piece of thin wire
- Lobster-style clasp
- Jump rings
- Crimp-style end findings
- Chain nose pliers

1. Unwind the cassette tape to make eight strips each 2 feet long. Tie the strips together at one end.

2. Attach a binder clip to the knot and pull the strips up through the Weave Wheel center.

3. Separate each strip and secure them in the slots so that they lie on both sides of 8, 16, 24, and 32.

4. Hold the Weave Wheel upright and remove the strip to the right of 32 (between 32 and 1).

5. Bring it down and secure it between 14 and 15.

6. Remove the strip between 16 and 17.

7. Bring it up and secure it between 31 and 30.

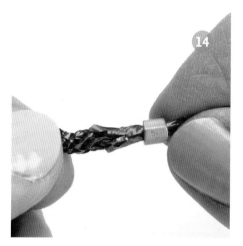

8. Rotate the wheel counterclockwise so that so that 8 is now at the top.

9. Continue by moving the strip between 8 and 9 and securing it between 22 and 23.

10. Then move the strip between 24 and 25 and secure it between 6 and 7.

    Again, rotate the wheel counterclockwise and repeat the pattern of placing the strips and rotating the wheel a quarter turn each time.

11. To add beads along the way, remove all of the strips from the wheel. Fold a wire over the strips to make a bead needle to easily thread the beads onto the tape.

12. Add a bead over the wire and gently slide it over the tape ends.

13. Pull the tape through the bead with your fingers to avoid stretching or breaking the tape strands.

14. Slide the bead up to the woven work. Add more beads if desired, or reattach the strips to the wheel to keep weaving.

15. To reattach the strips to the wheel after adding beads, remove the wire, then pull the strips up through the center and secure them into the slots as you did to begin the project. It is not necessary to put each strip in the same position it was in before, you can start fresh each time by placing the strips in the home position mentioned in step 3. Stop working when you are pleased with the length. To finish, use chain nose pliers to attach a crimp finding to each end. Use a jump ring to attach the lobster-style clasp to one of the crimp findings. Attach a jump ring to the other crimp finding to serve as the catch for the clasp.

UPCYCLED PLASTICS GALLERY

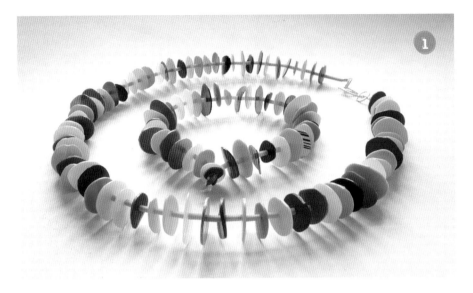

1. *Medium Disk Necklace and Bracelet* by Rebecca Crawford. Recycled plastic. Photo by the artist.

2. *Frosty Flower Necklace* by Rebecca Crawford. Recycled plastic. Photo by the artist.

3. *Multi-colored Bead Necklace* made from discarded plastic bags Helle Jorgensen. Photo by the artist.

4. *Green 2 Liter Bottle Bracelet* by Steven James. Recycled plastic. Photo by the artist.

5. *Spirograph Necklace* by Margot Potter. Vintage Spirograph wheels, old book pages, Ranger alcohol inks sealed with Collage Pauge. Photo by the artist.

6. *Crocheted Plastic Bracelet* made from recycled plastic bags by Beth Todd. Photo by artist.

4

UPCYCLED GLASS AND CERAMICS

Working with Recycled Glass and Ceramics

Creating jewelry with recycled glass requires a few special tools and pieces of equipment, but the end result is worth it. With cold working techniques, glass shards can be transformed into beautiful faux sea glass. Broken china plates can be turned into heart-shaped pendants by cutting and grinding and then left as is or surrounded with silver bezels. Cold work, including grinding, drilling, and tumbling, can be used with various types of glass. They can all be handled similarly since you don't have to worry about things like the coefficient of expansion (COE) or fusing temperatures when you're using cold working methods. You can create stunning jewelry pieces with cold work alone.

Certain types of glass can be transformed with heat and fused in molds to make beautiful cast pieces. With an emphasis on reuse in the artistic community, new techniques are being explored for fusing and casting recycled glass to make household items, such as tiles, and other accessories, including jewelry. Casting and fusing does require some patience and experimentation because different types of glass vary in how they respond to heat. Working with recycled glass can be challenging as you may not know what type the glass is. So, it is important to keep an open mind and expect a few failures when experimenting with these new techniques.

CUTTING

To break shapes of glass, tile nippers are used to create initial shapes. These can be found at shops that carry tools for cutting tile or making mosaics. After a bit of practice, nipping the glass will be easy. The trick is to take off small pieces at a time and realize that rounding a corner is really just a series of small straight cuts. It's important to know that you won't get a perfectly refined shape with nipping alone; grinding is necessary to further refine shapes.

GRINDING AND DRILLING

For glass grinding and drilling, diamond-coated drill bits and grinders are necessary. When used in conjunction with water the diamond surface on the bit does a beautiful job of refining glass shapes. The water serves several purposes: it cools as it grinds, it reduces friction, and it keeps the dust down. The grinder will help you get shapes you cannot nip with tile cutters. To drill through glass, use a diamond-coated drill bit under water to make holes in glass. Patience is required as it sometimes takes a few minutes to finish, but the wait is worth it.

SAFETY CONSIDERATIONS

Safety must be top priority when working with glass, whether breaking, grinding, or drilling it. Always wear eye protection and protect your skin from shards of glass. It can fly around when you least expect it, and even touching it can cut you. Avoid breathing in any fine dust particles from glass. Wearing a dust mask is good practice to protect your respiratory system, especially when grinding.

Jodi McRaney-Rusho's Cobalt Spring Bracelet *is made from cast recycled glass. Photo by the artist.*

Joy Marie Jones used broken china to make her Victorian Garden Necklace.
Photo by the artist.

Tumbled Glass Pendants

Designed by Sherri Haab

I love sea glass, and since I live far from a coast this project grew from my desire to make my own. I transformed broken bottle pieces into beautiful pieces of faux sea glass by simply shaping and tumbling the pieces. This process gives you a chance to make pieces with custom shapes and colors that would be rare to find on shore. The finished glass pieces can be made into jewelry by using techniques such as bezel setting or by using simple stringing techniques as I did in this project.

Supplies

- Broken glass pieces from bottles
- Two heavy plastic bags
- Hammer
- Tile nippers
- Rubber or leather gloves
- Eye protection
- Glass grinder with diamond-coated bit
- Sponge and water
- Rotary tumbler
- Tumbling medium (*coarse silicon carbide*)
- Dremel with collet to fit drill bit

- Diamond-coated drill bit (*1.8 or 2 mm blunt nose type*)
- Small shallow container (*such as a baking dish or plastic food container*)
- Wooden block to drill on (*an old rubber stamp works well*)
- Nylon bead cord or leather cord
- Beads
- Charms
- Jump ring
- Clasp finding
- Jewelry cement

1. Place glass pieces in a double plastic bag to contain the glass as you break it with a hammer. Always wear gloves and eye protection, even if the glass is covered. Gently select and pick up pieces with gloved hand. Use tile nippers to nip off corners to give the shapes a softer edge, which will help to round the corners in the next step. Make sure you wear gloves and eye protection as you continue through cutting and grinding.

2. Use a glass grinder fitted with a diamond-coated bit to smooth and round the edges of the glass. Keep water on the bit with a sponge to lubricate it as you grind. Gloves will protect you from cutting your skin. If you do not own a grinder you can still tumble rough shapes.

3. After grinding around the edges of the pieces, place them in a rotary tumbler to give them a "sea glass" surface. Fill the tumbler about ⅔ to ¾ full of glass. If you don't have enough of your own refined pieces, add some rough glass pieces to fill the tumbler. Add about 4–6 heaping tablespoons of coarse silicon carbide

tumbling medium. Add water to the tumbler, leaving just a few shards of glass on the top layer exposed. There should be friction with the medium and glass with just enough water to help the pieces move as they tumble.

Let the pieces tumble in a safe place for several days. Follow the manufacturer's instructions for care, safety, and proper use of the tumbler. Check the pieces daily until you are satisfied with the surface of the glass. Look for a frosty matte look to mimic sea glass. If the mix is too thick add water, or if it is too thin and watery add a spoonful or two of carbide medium. After you check the progress of the glass, wipe and dry the edges of the container lid before replacing it. When the glass pieces are done, rinse them in a container of clean water. Pat dry. Do not wash the medium down the drain. Let it settle and pour the water off the top before drying the medium for reuse or dry disposal.

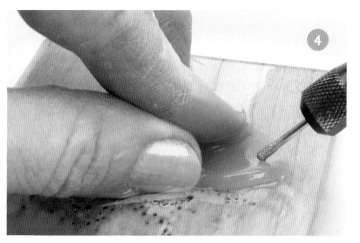

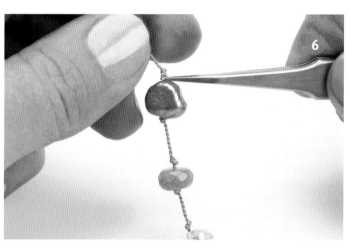

4. To drill a hole in the top of the glass to make a pendant, use a Dremel or other electric drill fitted with a diamond-coated drill bit. Drilling in water will help to lubricate and cool the piece, which will extend the life of the drill and keep the dust down. Place a wooden block in a shallow container of water. An old rubber stamp works well since the rubber grips the bottom of the container and steadies the block. (Hint: If you use a plain wooden block, a piece of wax or floral putty can be used to secure the block to the bottom of container.) Place the glass piece on the block with the water just deep enough to cover the surface of the glass. The drill bit itself is the only part of the drill that can be submerged; keep the rest of the drill out of the water for safety. Hold the piece of glass firmly on the wood block under water with your non-dominant hand. Turn the drill on at medium-high speed and nick the glass at a 45° angle to make a divot in the glass for the hole placement.

5. Without picking up the drill, slowly tilt the drill upright as it drills so that the bit is perpendicular to the glass. Let the bit continue to drill in the water. Only use light or medium pressure on the glass as you hold the drill. Too much pressure could break the bit. The hole may take a few minutes to drill, depending on how hard the glass is. As soon as the drill hits the wooden block the drill will sink into the wood readily. Be prepared to back off on the pressure and remove and turn the drill off as soon as you feel the drill "give" into the wood.

6. To string the sea glass, add a jump ring and a small charm and hang them from a leather cord, or use beads and nylon bead cord for a fancier look. To make a beaded cord, loop the center of the cord through the hole in the glass and then form knots along the cord to hold beads at intervals along the cord. Tweezers are helpful to hold each knot in place as you pull the cord; tweezers keep the knot close to the bead. Knot a clasp finding to each end of the beaded cord and seal cord ends with jewelry cement for a neat finish.

China Plate Charm

Designed by Sherri Haab

Broken china pieces can be turned into lovely keepsake jewelry pendants. China plates can be found in antique or thrift stores, or you may have a piece in your own collection that is chipped or broken. I like the fact that china often has colorful floral patterns with delicate designs that are just the right size for jewelry pieces. This is a project that has extra special value in that you can make it from dishes that hold family memories of days past.

Supplies

- Patterned stoneware or china
- Wheeled nippers (*Mosaic Mercantile*)
- Safety glasses or goggles
- Rubber or leather gloves
- Felt-tipped marker
- Chipper nippers (*Mosaic Mercantile*)
- Glass grinder with ¾" and ¼" diamond bits
- Wet sponge
- Copper adhesive tape (*stained-glass supplier*)
- Burnishing tool or bone folder
- Small pointed scissors
- X-Acto knife
- Ceramic tile or brick
- Sponge
- Soldering iron
- Paste or gel flux (*stained-glass supplier*)
- Flux brush

- Silver-bearing solder (*lead-free, jewelry grade*)
- Metal pan or cookie sheet
- Two pair of pliers
- Sterling silver jump rings
- Window cleaner
- Paper towel
- Steel wool
- Silver polish
- 24-gauge half-hard sterling silver wire
- Sterling silver chain
- Clasp
- Wire cutters
- Round nose pliers
- Chain nose pliers
- Assorted beads (*glass crystal, pearls, rhinestone balls*)
- Head pins to make bead dangles

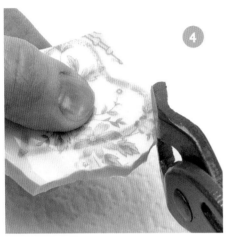

1. Hold the plate and use wheeled nippers held perpendicular to the edge of the plate to split the plate apart. The break line will follow the angle of the edge of the nippers, so aim the nippers to cut off to one side if you want to preserve a design in the center of the plate. To nip, clamp the wheels at the edge with a hard squeeze, holding one side of the plate to snap it apart. Wear leather or rubber gloves to protect your skin from glass edges as you cut. Always wear eye protection.

2. Use wheeled nippers to cut the next piece of the plate as though it were a pie wedge.

3. Make another break or two until you have a smaller piece of china (you are aiming for a small triangle shape). Draw a heart shape on the china with a felt-tipped marker. Use the wheeled nippers to cut small sections of china around the edge. The nippers will only make straight cuts, so don't try to follow the line around the curves of the heart shape or you will break the heart in half. Simply cut a triangle shape of glass following roughly around the line.

4. Chipper nippers are handy for trimming off small pieces and refining the shape. Cut off small pieces of china, chipping away to avoid breaking the entire piece.

5. After nipping, form the heart shape using a glass grinder with a wet sponge behind the diamond-coated bit. Wear rubber gloves to help you grip and form the sharp edges of the glass. Wear your hair tied back if you have long hair, and remember to wear eye protection. Grind around the edges following your marked shape. To form the dip in the center of the heart, hold the shape next to the bit and let it grind the shape. Switch to a ¼-inch diamond-coated bit to grind smaller heart shapes or to make the dip more pronounced. Keep the sponge behind the bit moist to reduce friction, heat, and dust.

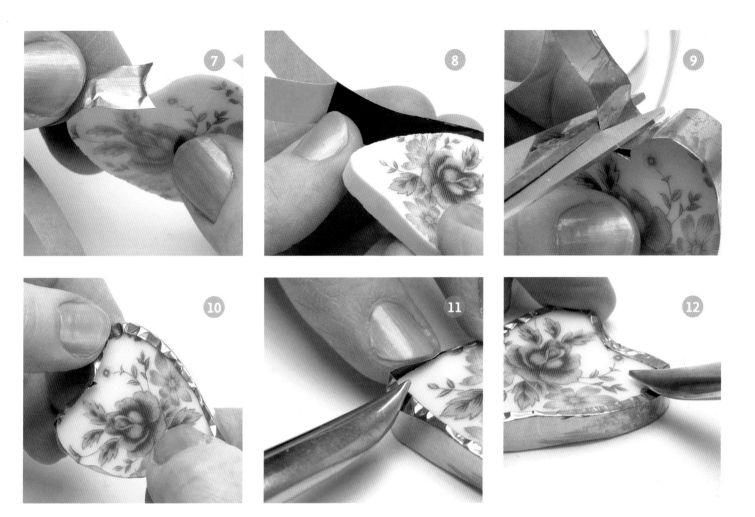

6. Clean off the dust and check the edges to make sure you are happy with the shape. Now you are ready to add the copper tape around the edge prior to soldering. China can vary in width, so check the width of your tape so that it will fold nicely just over the edge. To fit the tape around the shape make a V cut at the end of the tape with small pointed scissors to fit in the dip of the heart.

7. Remove the backing from the end of the tape and press the end of the tape down at the center of the dip.

8. Press the sticky side of the tape around the edge of the heart, removing the backing as you go, making sure to keep it centered, and preventing it from folding or tearing as you work.

9. When you have wrapped all the way around the edge, finish by overlapping slightly at the dip and cutting off the tape.

10. Smooth the tape around and over the edges with your fingers. Try the best you can to make small even pleats rather than big folds in the tape. This can be challenging around curves, and you may have a few folds.

11. When folding the tape over at the point of the heart use a burnishing tool or bone folder to fold one corner in first and then lap the other side over for a neat finish.

12. Burnish the tape down as flat as possible on the front and back of the heart using a metal burnishing tool or a bone folder.

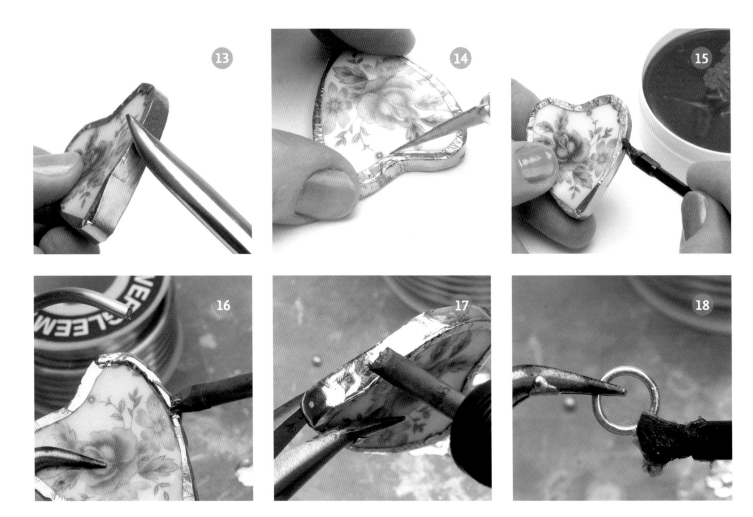

13. Burnish around the sides well.

14. Trim away excess tape sticking out at the dip of the heart with an X-Acto knife.

15. Cover all of the copper tape with flux using a brush. Flux is your friend, so cover the tape well to ensure that the solder will flow.

16. Set up a space to solder on a heat-proof surface, such as a ceramic brick or tile. Use a metal pan or cookie sheet to work on. Have a wet sponge at hand while you solder. Heat the soldering iron and position a length of lead-free solder by unwinding some from the spool so that a portion of the wire is suspended within reach of the iron over the piece you are soldering. Hold the china piece firmly with pliers. Heat the solder that is suspended from the roll over the tape and use the iron to melt and float the solder along the tape by moving the iron along.

Stroke the iron along the solder, allowing it to flow while moving it along instead of scraping or dragging the iron over the tape and you will make a neater and thicker bead of solder. Solder the front and back edges first. Use the sponge to clean the iron tip between strokes. Cool the piece before repositioning the pliers to move around the shape.

17. Solder around the side edges of the heart. Solder flows with gravity, so keep the piece upright where you are soldering. If you need to neaten the edges, you may need to apply more flux and then reheat and float the solder to smooth it along the edge.

18. To add a silver jump ring for hanging, place the heart in a vise or hold firmly with pliers so your hands will be free to solder the ring to the top. Brush flux over the seam of the jump ring.

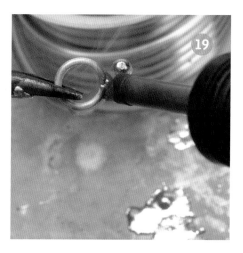 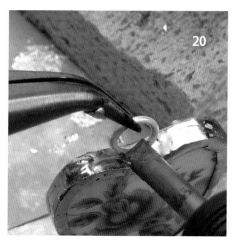 

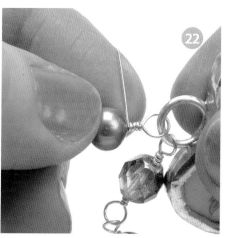 

19. Brush flux on top of the heart over the solder as well. Hold the jump ring in pliers and tin it by heating a bead of solder onto the jump ring over the seam.

20. Use the pliers to hold the jump ring firmly in place at the top of the heart. Heat the base of the jump ring and the solder below until it flows and then the jump ring will sink into place as you hold it in position. Make sure there is enough solder to flow over the ring to capture the ring in the solder. Add more solder if needed, using lots of flux.

21. After the piece is cool, wash off the flux with window cleaner and a paper towel. Use a piece of steel wool to remove the oxidation from the jump ring until the silver ring is shiny. Polish the silver if desired with a commercial polish.

22. To make the necklace, use sterling silver wire to make beaded segments using wrapped loops (see page 14) to connect the wires. Add chain and a clasp. Loop a beaded wire around the jump ring on the heart to attach. Finish by wrapping the end of the wire at the base of the loop.

23. Clip off the excess wire close to the wrap with wire cutters. Add bead dangles using head pins if desired. Add beads to the head pins, form loops, and wrap to attach to the chain.

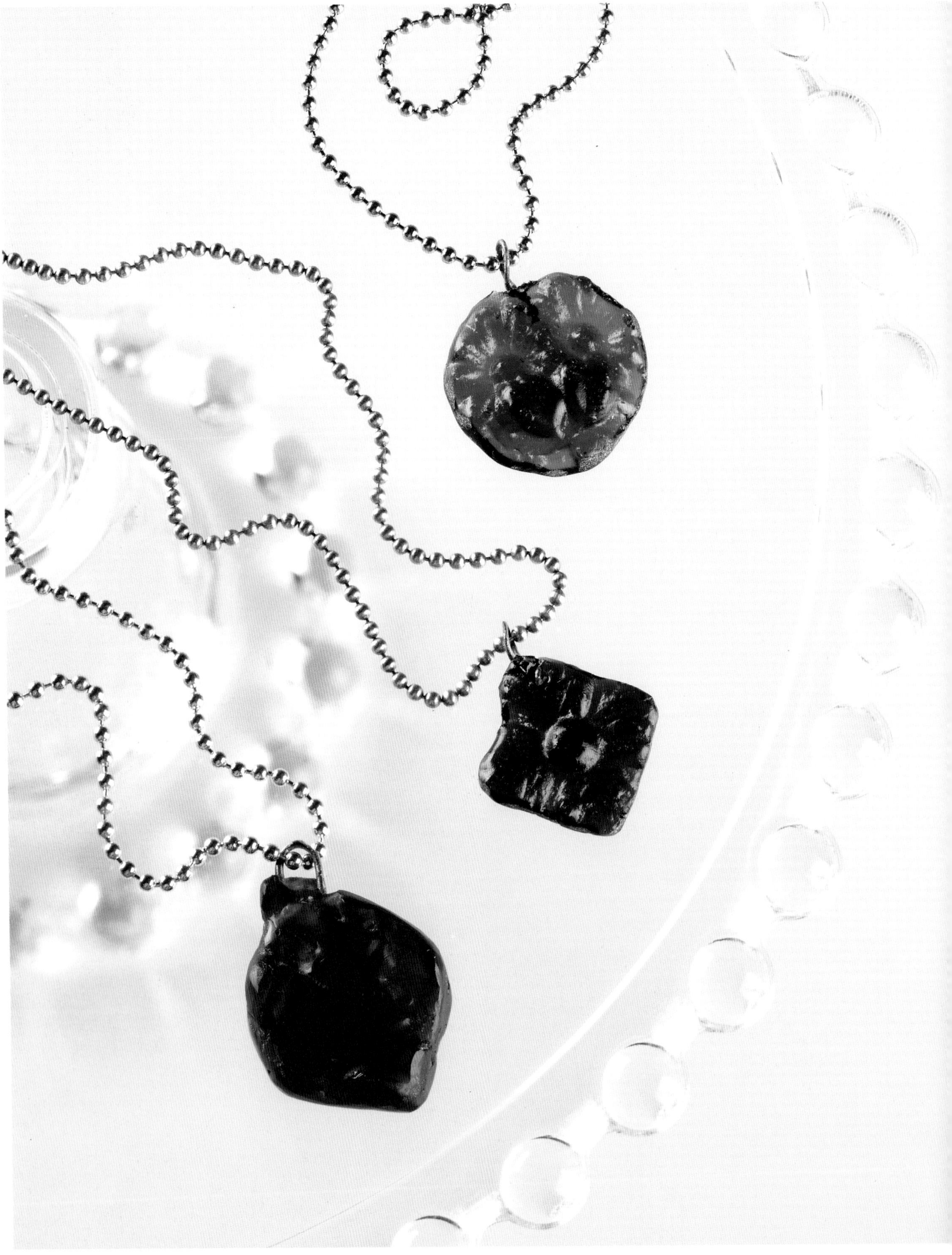

Molded Fused Glass Pendant

Designed by Bill Hess

Bill is the owner and founder of Ideas on Legs. Through his business he creates art and products that use recycled glass in new ways to emphasize sustainable and ecological design. He comments, "I have been experimenting with recycled glass for several years and thoroughly enjoy discovering new ways to create provocative art and craft pieces. In using this glass, I am adding soul and material history to the work while making a statement that is more mindful of the earth's resources."

Experimentation may be necessary to fuse the glass you are using since bottle glass is different than the glass that is sold and used for craft and jewelry purposes. Fusing recycled glass is difficult to master—but the results are worth it!

Supplies

- Purchased or handmade mold that is compatible with recycled glass
  - Option 1: Ceramic mold for recycled glass (*Jodi McRaney, Rusho Molds*)
  - Option 2: Mold-making kit (*greenglasscast.com*)
  - Option 3: Creative Paperclay or white ceramic earthenware clay (*for making your own mold*)
- Shell, large button, or other object (*for making your own mold*)
- Kiln wash
- Paint brush
- Lily Kiln Traveler (*Metal Clay Supply*)
- Clean glass bottles in clear, brown, green, and blue
- Old towel or rag (*big enough to wrap around a bottle*)
- Hammer
- Rubber or leather gardening gloves
- Protective eyewear

- Dust mask
- Small plates, trays, or cups (*for holding crushed glass*)
- Spoon
- 18-gauge copper wire (*1½ inch*)
- Creative Paperclay
- Needle nose pliers
- Wire cutter
- Glass grinder with diamond-coated drill bit
- Sponge
- Diamond-coated sanding blocks (*400, 800, and 1000 grit*)
- Belt sander (*Delta Porter Cable*)
- Cork belt for wet sanding (*150-, 220-, 400-, 600-grit cork belts*)
- Polishing oil
- Fine steel wool
- Purchased ball chain for hanging the pendant

1. Use a purchased mold that is rated for high firing temperatures that are suitable for recycled glass, or make your own mold. If you choose to make your own mold you can either purchase a kit or make a press mold. To make a clay press mold, choose an object that has a shallow relief and simple design, such as a seashell or a large button. Avoid complicated designs with protrusions, which can cause undercuts in the mold. Undercuts will cause the glass to stick in the mold, making the glass difficult to remove and resulting in a broken mold. Form small molds using Paperclay or earthenware clay by pressing the model into a ball of the clay. Make sure the walls surround the object for a nice deep mold. Remove the object and let the mold dry. Dry the molds well and then pre-fire in a kiln prior to filling with glass. Fire the earthenware type as directed for the type of clay you are using, or fire the Paperclay up to 1600°F, then turn off the kiln and let it cool before opening the door. Keep in mind that molds are fragile and not meant to hold up indefinitely. The molds will form cracks or break over time, and will need to be replaced.

2. Mix a small amount of kiln wash according to package directions and apply it to the inside of the molds. The kiln wash should dry quickly on the molds. Apply three coats with a brush, letting the wash dry between each coat. Place the molds on a kiln shelf that has been treated with kiln wash, as well.

3. Put on protective eyewear and gloves. Wrap a glass bottle in a towel, place it on the floor or workbench, and use a hammer to break the glass into small pieces (this is a little subjective, depending on the look you want) less than ½ inch in size. Empty the crushed glass into a small tray or cup. Do this for each bottle, keeping each color separate and being sure to carefully shake out the towel into the garbage between each use. Spoon the glass pieces into the prepared mold, trying to use the larger chunkier pieces of glass. Some glass artists screen the glass to separate the fine crushed glass from the chunks. Fill the mold with a mound that is higher in the center. Overfill the mold, so the glass will lose volume as it melts down into the mold.

Glass is rated in terms of coefficient of expansion (COE), and the COE varies depending on the type of glass. Art glass typically has a COE of 90–94. Common bottles in green, brown, and clear glass with a COE of 85–87 are used in this project. It is not advisable to mix different types of glass as the glass could break due to the differences in the expansion of glass. The COE also affects the fusing temperature of the glass.

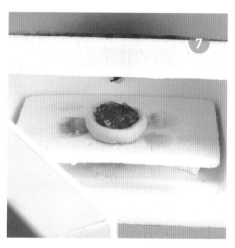

4. Using a wire cutter cut a 1½-inch length of copper wire for simple loop, or use a longer piece of wire for more complex shaped loop. Using the needle nosed pliers, form the loop or hook with the wire to embed in the glass.

5. Cover the loop portion of the wire that will not be embedded in the glass with a piece of Paperclay to keep the oxygen from the wire and avoid firescale (an oxidation layer on the wire).

6. Embed the wire into the glass at the edge of the mold, making sure there is glass under and over it. The loop will fire in place.

7. Carefully put the kiln shelf with the filled mold into the kiln, adjusting any glass that may have shifted to be sure the mold is filled and the embedded portion of the copper wire is covered.

KILN DIRECTIONS

The following directions are for a small electric kiln. Always keep kiln shelf paper or kiln wash on a shelf to protect your kiln from glass that might go astray. Turn on the kiln to fire the glass with the following program (this is a basic schedule for small jewelry-sized pieces that are at least ¼" thick):

- Heat the kiln at a ramp speed of 300°F/hour up to 1600°F. (This is an average temperature for recycled glass; you may need to fire 100°F higher or lower. Experiment with the glass you are using.)
- Hold for 20 minutes.
- Ramp down quickly (or crash cool by opening the door) to 1000°F.
- Close the door (if opened) and hold at 1000°F for 20–30 minutes to anneal the glass.
- Let the kiln cool down naturally without opening the door.

8. After the kiln has cooled, open the door. Remove your creations from the molds. Be careful when handling the work, as there will likely be some sharp areas.

9. Crumble the clay off of the copper loops and use steel wool to clean any firescale on the surface of the wires.

10. Put on protective eyewear, dust mask, and gloves. Begin cold working by grinding off any obvious pieces that would be structurally fragile or sharp points with a grinder fit with a diamond-coated bit. Keep water on the bit with a sponge to lubricate as you grind. Be sure to avoid marring the copper loop as you grind. After grinding, move on to sanders and polishers. Use progressively higher-numbered abrasives with the corresponding tool to smooth the edges of the piece. This photo shows a diamond-coated sanding block. For more shine, use progressive grits of cork on a belt sander. Polishing oil can be sprayed on the sanding belts to prolong the life of the abrasives and reduce dust and heat (which can cause cracking in the glass). Thread the finished pendant onto the chain through the loop.

UPCYCLED GLASS
AND CERAMICS GALLERY

1. *Antique Lace & French Limoges Broken China Necklace* by Joy Marie Jones. Photo by the artist.

2. *Silver Spoon Bracelet with Antique Wedgwood Broken China Charm* by Joy Marie Jones. Photo by the artist.

3. *Recycled Wood and Cast Glass Cuff Bracelets* by Jodi McRaney-Rusho. Photo by the artist.

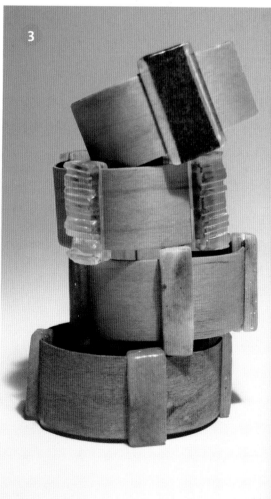

5

UPCYCLED
FABRIC AND
LEATHER

Working with Recycled Fabric and Leather

Soft materials, including wool, fabric, and leather, are very accessible and make nice jewelry-making materials. Recycle your own clothes or look for thrift shop finds. To find leather in a thrift shop, look and feel the belts and purses and look at the labels. You will find a few leather gems among all the vinyl. Belts and purse straps have finished edges and decorative stitching details that are perfect for a cuff-style bracelet. Using these materials is economical as well as being mindful of using recycled items for jewelry making. By adding metal hardware and traditional jewelry findings to these materials, it's very easy to assemble them into mixed media designs that are expressive and very stylish.

CUTTING

For wool and fabric, use good sewing scissors to cut the material. Cut leather with a good pair of scissors made specifically for leather. Leather punches and eyelet-setting tools will be helpful as well for leather and other fiber materials. A clean edge set with eyelets will give the piece a finished look.

SEWING

Sewing techniques apply to fabric and leather materials; thread, needles, and the like are simple to use to construct pieces. Sewing notions such as old buttons make clever closures for jewelry made of fabric or wool. Fabric adhesives and sealants can be found in fabric stores and can be used in addition to sewing techniques to make attachments or to finish raw edges.

Lisa Kettell uses leather from a recycled baseball, pearl beads, fiber, and rhinestones to create her Leather Cuff Bracelet. *Photo by the artist.*

Erin DeLargy (Hot Pink and Sequins) upcyles hand-dyed leather to create her **Pretty Poppies Necklace.** *Photo by the artist.*

T-shirt Rose Jewelry

Designed by Michelle Haab

Many of us save favorite T-shirts for sentimental reasons, even after they are worn out. Michelle had a bunch of old T-shirts that were dear to her, and this project gave her a way to justify keeping them. She cut up her old T-shirts and gave them a new life by turning them into funky fabric rose jewelry designs.

For a simple pin, make one single rose to wear on a new T-shirt or sweater. If you are ambitious, make an arrangement of roses for a spectacular blooming necklace.

Supplies for pin
- Old T-shirts or fabric
- Hot glue gun
- Fabric scissors
- Felt
- Tulle
- Pin back finding

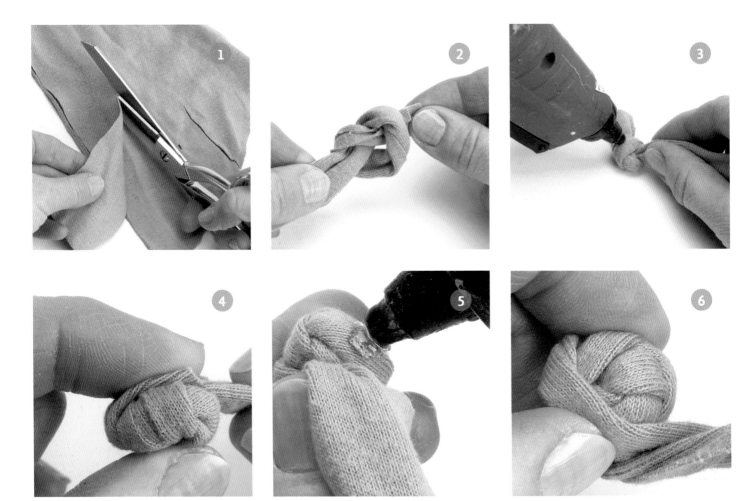

1. Cut up a T-shirt to use the fabric for the roses. Cut strips 2 inches wide from the sleeves or body of the shirt, cutting with the grain of the fabric.

2. Fold the strip in half lengthwise and tie a knot toward one end of the strip and pull tightly. The knot will be used to form a rosebud shape.

3. Put a single drop of hot glue on the back of the knot, which will be used to glue the short end of the strip in place in the next step.

4. Glue the short tail of the fabric onto the back of the knot and wrap the longer end of the strip over the short piece to conceal it. This will hide the short end of the strip neatly to prevent frayed edges from showing.

5. Wrap the strip around the outside of the knot in a spiral. Use single drops of hot glue sparingly to hold the strips in place.

6. Continue to work the strip around the rose to make the rose larger as you wrap.

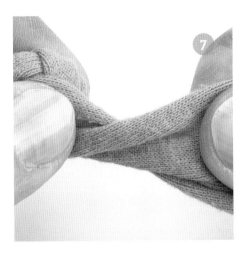

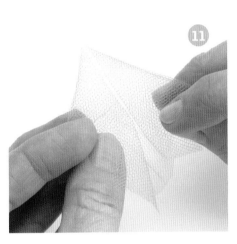

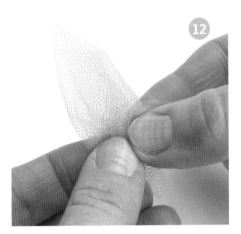

7. Add a twist every so often to add dimension to your rose.

8. When reaching the end of the strip, if you would like to add another strip of fabric to make a larger rose, work the strip in by tacking it almost perpendicular over the end of the first strip. This will create the illusion of a twist and appear as a continuous strip. Continue your revolutions.

9. To add tulle, hot glue the end of the tulle underneath or inside the strip you are about to wrap so that you can wrap both together as though they were one strip. The fabric will hold the tulle in place as you wrap both around.

10. While holding the tulle in place, use your other hand to continue wrapping the fabric to secure the tulle.

11. When the rose reaches the size you want, use hot glue to secure the final revolution. Fold the remaining fabric underneath the rose and secure with glue. Cut off the excess. To make a tulle leaf, cut a small square and fold in half crosswise. Fold the corners in to make a point.

12. Gather the base of the tulle to make a leaf shape.

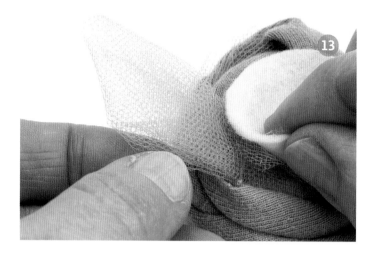

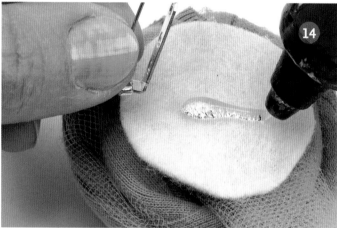

13. Glue the leaf to the back of the rose. Cut out an appropriately sized felt circle for the backing and attach with hot glue.

14. Attach a pin back to the felt circle with more hot glue.

Variation: BLACK AND WHITE T-SHIRT ROSE NECKLACE

To make a cluster of roses for a full necklace design, simply hot glue finished roses together, adding leaves of tulle to form a pleasing design. The glue is applied to the sides of the roses, and then the roses are pushed together firmly to hold as the glue sets. Glue a braided cord made of tulle or T-shirt strips to make a necklace cord to whatever length suits you. Simply tie a bow to fasten the necklace.

Felted Sweater Pins

Designed by Rachel Haab

If you've ever accidentally tossed a wool sweater in the washing machine you probably got quite a surprise when your sweater, which once fit, came out small enough for a toddler. Although you did not plan on it, you experienced the technique of felting. Through water, heat, and agitation, wool fibers interlock and become very dense and compact. This is how felt is made. This technique can be used intentionally to prepare wool to be recycled into jewelry pieces. The increased density of the wool is perfect for structure in a design. These flower pins were designed to use small scraps from various weights of wool. The patchwork design celebrates the fact that they were recycled. As a costume designer, Rachel loves collecting fabrics and was drawn to this project because it is a fun way to make use of wool scraps.

Supplies
- 100% wool sweaters in various colors
- Mesh garment bag
- Fabric scissors
- Beading needle
- Thread
- Small seed beads
- Pin back finding
- Hot glue *(optional)*

1. Place the sweaters in a mesh garment bag and wash in hot water in a washing machine. This mesh bag will help reduce the amount of loose fibers that are filtered through the washing machine. Rinse with cold water. Dry the sweaters on a hot cycle to felt the wool as much as possible. Cut sections from the sweater using fabric scissors.

2. Cut out a flower shape for the background piece of the flower pin. Cut petal shapes from various pieces in different colors. Cut a round center piece for the flower. These shapes were cut freehand, but you can make a flower-shaped pattern of paper if you desire

3. Use a beading needle with thread to stitch the petals onto the background piece. Stitch the felt circle to the middle of the flower.

4. Stitch small seed beads around the edge of the petals using a whip stitch. A whip stitch brings the thread up out of the fabric, up over the edge, and then back up through the fabric. The thread captures the edge of the felt with each stitch.

5. Stitch beads around the center edge of the middle of the flower.

6. Stitch or hot glue a pin back finding to the back of the flower.

Purse or Belt Strap Cuff Bracelet

Designed by Sherri Haab

Belts and purse straps are perfect for making leather cuff bracelets—they are already a good width for cuff designs so the finished edges of the leather work to your advantage. I enjoy going to thrift stores and searching for quality leather among all the vinyl items. Recycled leather pieces cut from belts or purses not only save you money, they also save you work if you can find ways to implement the finished details of the leather.

Supplies
- Leather purse strap or belt
- Leather scissors
- A few inches of found chain pieces
- Eyelets to fit punched holes
- Eyelet tool punch (*Crop-A-Dile*)
- Hole punch
- Pronged metal embellishment (*Arte Metal Decorivets*)
- Chain nose pliers
- Metal clasp
- Jump rings

1. Use a leather belt or purse strap to make your cuff bracelet. Cut off a section to use and choose a pronged metal embellishment to attach to the center. Punch two holes in the leather using a small hole punch for the prongs corresponding with where they align. This photo shows the Crop-A-Dile tool, but you could use any small leather hole punch.

2. Place the prongs through the holes to attach the embellishment. A found chain was added to the sides of the embellishment over the prong prior to placing in the hole for decoration.

3. Crimp the prongs down on the backside of the leather with chain nose pliers.

4. Add another decorative pronged piece to each side of the chain segment. Attach the pieces to the leather in the same manner as you did in steps 2 and 3. Measure your wrist and subtract a little for the chain clasp. Use leather scissors to cut the bracelet to fit your wrist.

5. Punch two holes near each end of the bracelet for eyelets.

6. Push the eyelets in place.

7. Crimp the eyelets down with the Crop-A-Dile setter.

8. Use pliers to attach a chain segment or use a few jump rings to form a chain extending from each eyelet. Join the two chain segments on each side with one jump ring using chain nose pliers and add a clasp to finish the cuff.

Jean Label Jewelry

Designed by Sherri Haab

In my quest to find an easy source of leather to recycle, I only had to look as far as my own closet to find leather labels on the backs of jeans. With a few pair of outdated "mom" jeans to choose from, I found really cool leather labels with fancy graphics representing the makers and designers of the jeans. It was fun to think of the possibility of turning such an understated part of clothing into leather jewelry. The labels are easy to remove with a seam ripper and provide nice pieces to use for creating mixed media bracelets. If you can't find labels of your own, hopefully your teens or husband won't notice the dark blue square on the back of their jeans where the label used to be.

BLACK LABEL BRACELET WITH ROSE ORNAMENT

Supplies

- Seam ripper
- Scissors or leather shears
- 2–3 leather label patches cut from jeans
- Sizzix Big Shot die-cut machine
- Label- or tag-shaped die for Sizzix machine
- Eyelets
- Eyelet punch tool (*Crop-A-Dile*)
- Leather needle
- Heavy-duty thread
- Decorative button for closure
- Small flat button for counter button
- Leather or elastic cord
- White glue
- Gem-Tac glue
- Flat-backed decorative piece

Optional supplies for decorating bracelet edge

- Small leather punch tool or sharp leather needle
- Beading needle
- Small beads

1. Use a seam ripper or scissors to remove the leather labels from jeans.

2. Use a thin leather piece for the center of the bracelet. Cut it into a shape using a label- or tag-shaped die by rolling it through the Sizzix machine as directed by the manufacturer. This piece was cut from black leather, but you can use any color of leather you want.

   Cut two strips with scissors (or leather shears if the leather is thick) for each side of the bracelet from another leather label. Place each strip at the end of the black center label where you would like to attach it.

3. Punch two holes (⅛-inch size) on each end of the center piece with the Crop-A-Dile, punching through both layers of leather to make holes for eyelet attachments.

4. Place eyelets through the holes.

5. Set the eyelets with the Crop-A-Dile tool.

6. Measure the bracelet to fit and trim if necessary. Punch one hole (⅜ inch) on one end of the bracelet strips with the Crop-A-Dile tool to attach a cord loop. Set an eyelet in place with the same tool.

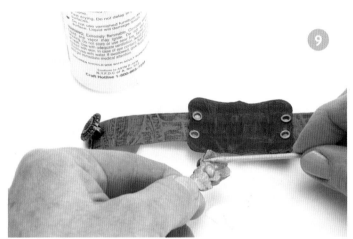

7. On the other end of the bracelet use a leather needle and thread to sew a decorative button with a shank on the back for the closure of the bracelet. Sew a flat counter button on the back, looping through both as you sew.

8. Form a loop with elastic or leather cord to fit over the button for the closure. Loop through the eyelet and tie square knots to secure the ends as shown. Add white glue to prevent fraying if using elastic.

9. Use Gem-Tac glue to attach a flat-backed decorative piece to the front of the bracelet. The piece in this project was an antique rose ornament with a flat back. Use any decorative piece as long as it has a flat surface on the back to allow it to be glued to the leather.

10. Press the ornament onto the leather. As an option, sew beads along the edge of the bracelet. Punch holes first using a sharp leather needle or small leather punch tool. Stitch beads in place with a beading needle passing it through the holes. Add a bead for each stitch.

Variation: BEE CUFF BRACELET

For a different look, cut a wide strip of leather from an old belt or purse and use this as the foundation of the bracelet and add a design in the form of an appliqué cut from a leather jean label. Use buttons or other embellishments to personalize the cuff.

Supplies

- Sizzix Big Shot die cut machine
- Sizzix Sizzlits bee die
- Leather jean label
- Leather cut from belt or purse
- Leather shears
- Crop-A-Dile tool
- Eyelets
- White glue
- Leather needle
- Heavy-duty thread
- Decorative buttons for closure
- Small flat buttons for counter buttons
- Leather or fabric adhesive
- Leather or round elastic for closure
- Headpins
- Beads for bead dangles
- Round nose pliers
- Chain nose pliers

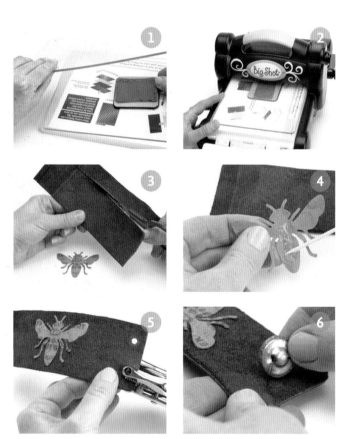

1. Place a thin leather label over the bee die and sandwich between acrylic as directed by manufacturer to cut shape.

2. Roll the die through the Big Shot machine to cut shape

3. Cut a wide strip of leather from a belt or old purse that is sized to fit your wrist to make a cuff bracelet.

4. Apply leather or fabric glue to the back of the bee shape and adhere to the center of the cuff.

5. Punch two holes on each side of the cuff with the Crop-A-Dile tool. Set eyelets in the holes with the same tool.

6. Sew two buttons on each side using a leather needle and heavy-duty thread; sew small counter buttons on back to keep the buttons from ripping the leather. Knot two loops of elastic or leather cord through the eyelets on the other end of the bracelet using square knots. Add white glue to keep the ends from fraying. See steps 7–9 from the Black Label Bracelet with Rose Ornament project for details on how to make this type of closure. Embellish the knots with bead dangles to add sparkle to the cuff.

UPCYCLED FABRIC AND LEATHER GALLERY

1. *Mixed Media Red Leather Cuff Bracelet* by Ruth Rae. Cuff made from recycled leather belt, etched copper and silver, recycled fibers. Photo by the artist.

2. *Poppy Pins* by Erin DeLargy (Hot Pink and Sequins). Hand-dyed upcycled leather. Photo by the artist.

3. *Button and Fabric Neckace* by Ruth Rae. Necklace made from old buttons and lace and fabric scraps. Photo by the artist.

6

UPCYCLED
FOUND
OBJECTS

Working with Found Objects

Found objects are any parts or pieces you find interesting enough to include in your jewelry. Using them is a way to reclaim even the most insignificant item and showcase it in a piece of jewelry. One of the magical uses of found objects is taking something that is discarded or rarely noticed and bringing it to life as an important element in a design. Jewelry is a nice way to display things that are often collected; it's a way to bring them out in the open to enjoy instead of keeping them hidden in a shoebox or sitting on a dusty shelf.

With found objects, anything goes. This is fun jewelry to make because you can combine various materials and create surprising results. It's a great way to recycle heirlooms, broken jewelry pieces, junk drawer items, and even small electronic parts. To incorporate found objects into jewelry, one can use a variety of techniques to assemble the piece. Cold connections such as rivets and wire attachments are good ways to make attachments. Fiber and sewing techniques can also be used. If the pieces have loops or holes, it's easy to sew or wire things together. In addition to making cold connections, adhesives like epoxy resin and resin clay can be useful as a way to provide a setting or protective covering for small objects you wish to feature. Many of the techniques used in other projects in the book can be borrowed and applied to found objects, so it's only a matter of determining the way you want to work with the material at hand.

EPOXY RESIN

Epoxy resin is available in many formulations and is used for a variety of applications. People most often think of it as a glue or surface coating, but it can also be used to form solid castings.

All epoxy resins are similar in the sense that the resin must be mixed with a catalyst to harden or cure. Most are formulated to be mixed in a 1:1 ratio, which makes measuring easy. The two parts are poured into a cup and stirred. It is important that care be taken to mix carefully and completely for proper curing. After the resin is mixed it begins to catalyze. After mixing it can be poured into molds or bezels. Different types cure at different rates, ranging from minutes to hours. Clear coating resin is one type of two-part resin and is used in the Found Tin Bezel Toy Ring project (see page 129) to encapsulate small objects in a bezel.

The same principle for mixing applies to quick-setting epoxy, which is extruded from a two-part tube. This type of resin is much thicker than liquid resin. It is used to attach jewelry findings to a hard surface such as attaching a ring blank as shown in the Found Found Tin Bezel and Tiny Toy Ring project. Mix equal parts with a toothpick on a piece of wax paper.

RESIN CLAY

A new type of resin is available in the form of clay, which is mixed like putty to produce colorful solid plastic pieces. The Resin Clay Electronic Scrap Ring project (see page 137) uses this type of clay resin. Resin clay is also mixed in two parts. The clay is kneaded together until well mixed. It will air cure into a hard plastic without requiring heat, which makes it an excellent choice for embedding objects such as plastic or other non-heat-proof materials.

SAFETY CONSIDERATIONS

Regardless of the type of resin used you should always follow safety precautions. Wear rubber gloves and respiratory gear, such as a mask for vapors and fumes, and work in a well-ventilated area.

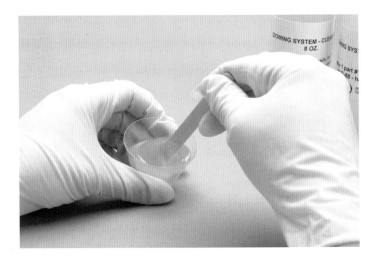

Mix two-part epoxy coating resin thoroughly in a small cup using a craft stick.

Nihal Dölek used recycled metal zippers and a vintage button to create her Vintage Zipper Pendant Necklace. *Photo by the artist.*

Amanda Preske used circuit board parts, resin, and a silver-plated bezel to create her Wordy Circuit Pendant. *Photo by the artist.*

Stamped Metal and Found Object Necklace

Designed by Shannon Porter

Shannon has a knack for design and putting unusual things together in aesthetically pleasing patterns. Her fond memories of her father inspired this necklace. "My dad has always been a collector of junk—old car parts, signs, bottles, and much more. While trying to get my craft space together, I went rummaging through my dad's old barn to look for wooden boxes to store tools in and old bottles to hold beads. An old bottle caught my eye, and I was instantly inspired with a jewelry design. Then I found an old boot accessory to go with it. Old barns and rusty antiques have always been my favorite things because they remind me of the 'junk-hunting excursions' I went on with my dad as a little girl." Shannon's project features stamping on metal to personalize the necklace with words or phrases. Patina is used to darken the letters for more contrast.

Supplies

- Scraps of copper or other metal to stamp on *(24-gauge or thinner for best results)*
- Metal shears
- Steel block
- Steel letter stamps
- Hammer
- Patina solution
- Cotton swab
- Polishing pad or cloth
- Metal punch
- Small bottle

- 24- or 26-gauge sterling silver wire *(round half-hard)*
- Tape
- Beads to fit over wire
- Chain nose pliers
- Round nose pliers
- Metal file
- Sandpaper
- Wire cutters
- Crimping pliers
- Sterling silver clasp
- Decorative dangles and beads

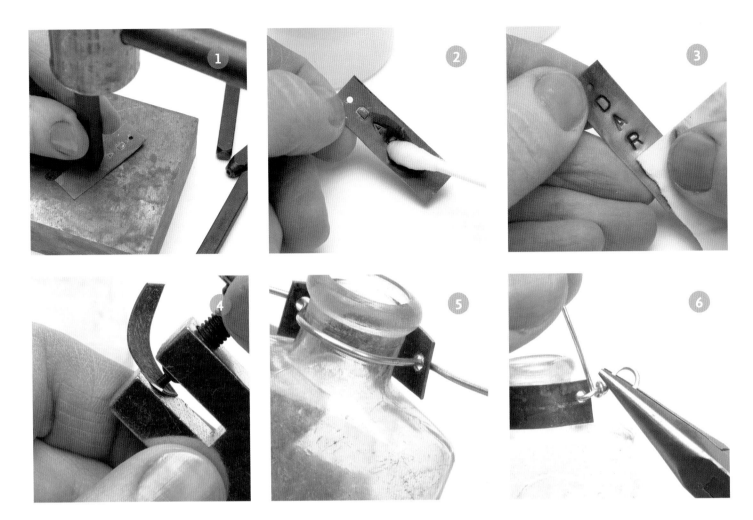

1. Cut a small strip of metal to stamp a word onto. Place the strip on a steel block and use steel letter stamps and a hammer to strike the letters onto the metal.

2. File or sand the edges if necessary. Use a swab to apply patina solution to the surface of the stamped metal.

3. After the patina solution has dried, rinse with water and then buff the patina off the raised areas with a polishing cloth. The patina will remain in the recessed areas.

4. Use a metal punch to make a hole at each end of the strip of the metal.

5. Wrap a wire around the neck of the bottle and thread through the holes in the metal to attach the piece.

6. Make a loop with round nose pliers on each side and wire wrap at the base of the loop.

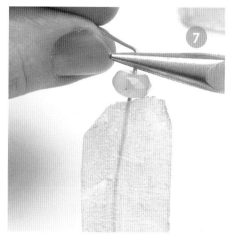

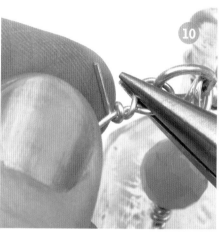

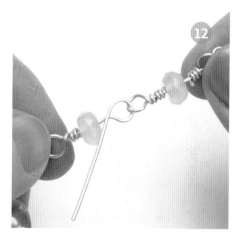

7. Cut a length of wire to begin building wire segments to form the necklace. A piece of tape adhered to the wire helps to hold the bead on the wire as you form the first loop. Use chain nose pliers to bend the wire above the bead to begin the loop.

8. Form a loop with the bent wire with round nose pliers, making sure not to wrap until the attachment is made in the next step.

9. Attach a wire with a formed loop to the bottle to begin adding bead segments.

10. Wrap the wire at the base of the loop.

11. Use crimping pliers to control the wire as you tuck the end of the wire in at the base of the wrap. The jaws of the pliers have a channel that will help you crimp down over the wire to accomplish a neat wrap.

12. Continue linking segments using loops and wire wraps until you are happy with the length of the necklace.

13. Clip off the ends of the wire with wire cutters after wrapping the wire at the base of each loop. Add a clasp with chain nose pliers to finish the necklace.

14. Add decorative elements such as dangles and beads.

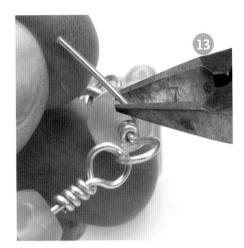

Variation: BEADED EARRINGS

Follow steps 1-4 for the necklace to make a stamped metal strip for each earring. Attach a beaded head pin dangle to each earring with a wire-wrapped loop, and then attach ear wires using chain nose pliers.

Additional Supplies

- Two copper rectangle strips for earrings
- Two ear wires
- Two beads
- Two head pins

Found Tin Bezel and Tiny Toy Ring

Designed by Rachel Haab

Small figurines were commonly found in hobby stores in days past. They were used for model train scenes, cake decorations, and for tiny scenes inside blown eggs. These old pieces are fun to hunt for in antique stores. They are often incredibly detailed, and using them to make a kitschy ring is a great way to recycle them. The ring base can be made from a small vintage tin or even a metal bottle cap. Inside you can use paper, glitter, and small model figurines or small toys to create scenes. A two-part doming epoxy resin fills the bezels to preserve the scene inside to finish the rings.

Supplies

- Small tins or metal container
- Small toys or figurines
- Old postcards, paper, ephemera
- Scissors
- Mod Podge decoupage glue
- White glue
- Toothpick
- Two-part epoxy doming resin *(Ice Resin, Objects and Elements)*
- Mixing cups and craft stick for mixing resin
- Wax paper
- Small paint brush
- Ring blank
- Quick-setting two-part epoxy resin
- Embossing heat tool
- 200- or 320-grit sandpaper
- Nitrile rubber gloves

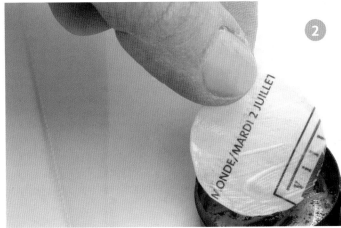

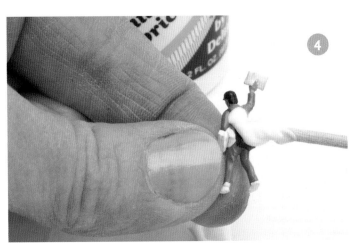

1. Choose a tin that is small enough to use for your ring face and choose small toys or figurines to display in it. Choose a paper that will complement it to serve as the background. Cut a paper shape to fit inside the tin. Coat the front and back and side edges of the paper with Mod Podge to seal the paper. Work on wax paper so the paper won't stick to your work surface. Let the glue dry well. This will prevent the resin from staining the paper.

2. Place the paper in the tin using a layer of Mod Podge to adhere.

3. Use a toothpick to tuck the edges of the paper in around the inside of the tin.

4. Apply white glue to the back of the small figure and glue into the tin.

5. After the glue has dried, mix the two-part epoxy doming resin according to the manufacturer's instructions. Work in a well-ventilated area and wear nitrile rubber gloves to protect skin. Fill the tin with the mixed resin.

6. To remove bubbles from the resin you can heat the resin from straight overhead with an embossing heat tool. Be careful not to blow the resin over the edge. Working in a warm environment will also reduce bubbles. Let the resin cure for at least 24 hours in a warm place.

7. After the resin is cured, use quick-setting two-part epoxy resin to attach a ring blank finding. Sand the pad of the blank prior to gluing for better adhesion. Keep the ring blank level as it cures so that the blank will not slide. Let it cure 24 hours.

Sewing Snap Jewelry

Designed by Rachel Haab

Rachel is a seamstress and costume designer. Sewing supplies and notions appeal to her, and she is especially fond of vintage notions. She used her beading skills to construct a bold repetitive design with black snaps. By featuring snaps as the main material of her design she is celebrating using functional parts that are usually hidden in a garment. To make matching earrings, simply add ear wires and bead dangles. This project also teaches you how to make your own matching jump rings using common wire.

Supplies for bracelet

- 36 black sewing snaps *(9 mm size)*
- 22-gauge black galvanized wire
- Wooden dowel or skewer *(approximately 3.5–4 mm in thickness)*
- Flush side cutters *(you may want use an old pair as galvanized wire can damage fine cutters)*
- Two pair chain nose pliers
- Black hook-and-eye closure

1. The design consists of two rows of snaps connected with jump rings. You can use purchased jump rings or make your own. To make your own jump rings, cut off about 12 inches of wire and wrap the wire evenly around a wooden dowel or skewer to form a coil.

2. Slide the coil from the dowel and clip off the end of the wire. Make sure you have a flush cut (clean flat cut) for both ends of wire to form the jump ring. The flat side of the cutter will give you a flush cut, so always keep this side facing the end of each ring as you cut the jump rings.

3. To make the next cut to complete the jump ring, flip the cutters over so that the flush cut will be made on the opposite end of the ring. Now you will have a ring where both ends are flush, which will help the ends meet neatly when you close the ring with pliers. If you cut with the wrong side of the cutter you will see that the wire looks beveled or pointed. It helps to practice a few times.

4. The end of the remaining coil will now have a beveled cut which you will need to snip off to start a new jump ring.

5. Continue cutting the wire in this way to make a series of jump rings for the bracelet.

6. To assemble the snaps with the jump rings to form the bracelet, use two pair of chain nose pliers to close the jump rings as you add snaps to form a row.
   Add a second row of snaps, attaching the rows together with more jump rings.

7. After measuring for fit, finish by attaching a hook-and-eye closure to each end with jump rings.

Variation: SILVER SNAP BRACELET AND POST EARRINGS

The silver snap bracelet is made using just one row of snap with purchased silver jump rings. The silver earrings are made using eye closures as part of the dangle design. The earrings are a post style with a post pad findings attached to the back of the snap with quick-setting epoxy.

Supplies
- Silver snaps of various sizes (enough to form bracelet)
- Hook and eye for closure
- Silver colored jump rings

For earrings:
- Two snaps
- Two eye closures
- Two beads
- Two post earring finding with flat pad
- Quick-setting epoxy resin

Variation: SNAP DANGLE EARRINGS

For another earring variation simply add ear wires and bead dangles to larger snaps. See page 15 for information on how to make a dangle with a head pin.

Supplies
- Two large sewing snaps (1/2 inch or larger)
- Gunmetal-colored earwires
- Two head pins
- Two beads for dangles

Resin Clay Electronic Scrap Ring

Designed by Sherri Haab

My husband, Dan, is an engineer, so we always have a variety of small electronic parts on hand at home. It is fun, quick, and super-easy to recycle these high-tech electronic parts and make funky rings. Salvage small components from broken cell phones or other discarded electronics to embed in the clay to make the designs. Almost anything can be embedded in resin clay since baking is not required. The clay catalyzes after being mixed at room temperature. The parts generally do not require gluing since the clay is an adhesive in and of itself.

Supplies

- Broken cell phone or electronic parts to embed
- Two-part epoxy resin clay *(Apoxie Sculpt)*
- Ring blanks with open bezel
- Rubber gloves
- Tweezers

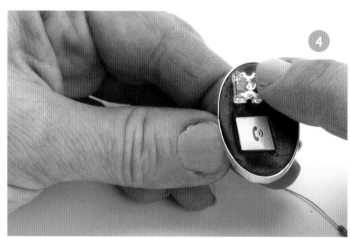

1. Select electronic pieces to use for your ring face. Do not use batteries in the design. Mix the two-part epoxy resin clay according to the manufacturer's instructions. Pay attention to safety guidelines and wear rubber gloves to prevent skin irritation while mixing.

2. When the clay is thoroughly mixed it is ready to press into the ring bezel. Press the clay into the bezel, shaping the surface as desired. It can be flat or domed. You can also texture the clay if you like.

3. Push small electronic parts into the clay. Push the clay around the parts to hold them securely embedded in the resin. The nice thing about resin clay is that you do not have to glue the parts, as the resin will act as an adhesive to hold them. The resin gives you about 30 minutes to an hour of working time before it starts to stiffen and eventually harden.

4. For extra small pieces use tweezers to embed the parts. Let the ring sit overnight before wearing.

Variation: ALL CLAY ELECTRONIC SCRAP RING

This ring can also be made entirely out of resin clay, which gives it a fresh, fun, modern look. Resin clay does not shrink much so the ring form can be built to size on a ring mandrel and will fit accurately after the clay cures. Once cured the ring will be sturdy as resin clay is incredibly strong.

Additional supplies
- Ring mandrel (Metal Clay Supply)
- Cellophane tape

1. To form a ring with the resin clay, wrap the clay around a ring mandrel of the desired finished size. To keep the clay from sticking to the mandrel, wrap the mandrel with a strip of a double layer of cellophane tape first. Cut two pieces of tape and place them with sticky sides together to ensure that one smooth side is against the mandrel and the other smooth side is in contact with the clay ring.

2. Wrap a snake of clay around the mandrel to make a ring. Press an electronic part into the center for decoration. Let the ring cure on the mandrel and remove the tape from the shank when set.

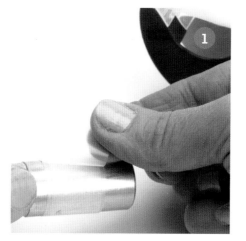
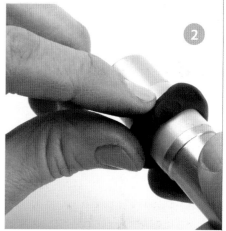

UPCYCLED FOUND OBJECTS GALLERY

1. *Sea Shell* by Stephanie Lee. Soldered bezel, wing-shaped seashell, mica, chain, bead. Photo by the artist.

2. *Superman Circuit* by Amanda Preske. Pendant circuit board parts, resin, silver-plated bezel. Photo by the artist.

3. *Spoon Necklace* by Stephanie Lee. Vintage mother-of-pearl button, silver spoon; wire wrapped and soldered. Photo by the artist.

4. *Ocean Blue Necklace* by Lika Schindler. Recycled jewelry parts—links from belt, silver brooch, vintage beaded earring. Photo by the artist.

5. *Yellow Cufflinks* by Amanda Preske. Circuit board parts, resin, silver-plated cufflink findings. Photo by the artist.

6. *Brownie Circuit Pendant Bezel* by Amanda Preske. Circuit board parts, resin, silver plated. Photo by the artist.

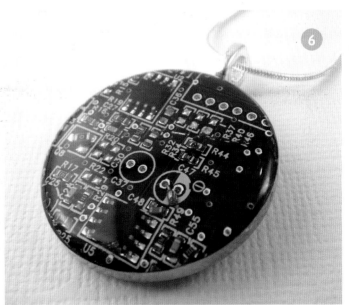

Contributing Artists

Rachel Haab
rachelhaab.com

Bill Hess
ideasonlegs.com

Steven James
macaroniandglitter.com

Shannon Porter
e-mail: oldriveraa@broadweave.net

Jane Salley
thejaneworld.com

Richard Salley
rsalley.com

Gallery Contributors

Heidi Borchers
ecoheidi.com

Rebecca Crawford
myspacefruit.com

Erin Delargy
hotpinkandsequins.com

Amy DeLeo (Ju Ju Beads)
jujubead.com

Nihal Dölek
nezjewelry.etsy.com

Steven James
macaroniandglitter.com

Joy Marie Jones
CupidsCharm.com

Helle Jorgensen
hellejorgensen.typepad.com

Lisa Kettell
moonfairesworld.com

Stephanie Lee
stephanielee.typepad.com

Susan Lenart Kazmer
susanlenartkazmer.net

Jodi McRaney-Rusho
glasswithapast.com

Margot Potter
margotpotter.com

Amanda Preske
beadworkbyamanda.etsy.com

Ruth Rae
ruthrae.com

Lika Schindler
ecoblingcouture.etsy.com

Beth Todd
bethtoddcreatz.etsy.com

Spoon It Over by Amy DeLeo. Photo by Todd Bliss.

Resources

Aves Studio (avesstudio.com)
Self-hardening epoxy resin clays, Apoxie Sculpt

Bailey Ceramic Supplies (baileypottery.com)
C-175-164 kiln wash (porcelanite)

Beaducation (beaducation.com)
Jewelry-making tools, online videos, jewelry findings

Burnt Offerings (burntofferings.com)
Jewelry-making tools, tin snips, metal punch, eyelets

Cat's Cradle Antiques & Art (168 W. Center St., Provo, UT 84601)
Unique jewelry pieces, vintage paper, antique glass

C. R. Laurence Co. Inc. (crlaurence.com)
Sanding tools and supplies for glass

Dad's Rock Shop (dadsrockshop.com)
Tumbling media for glass

Delphi Glass (delphiglass.com)
Tile nippers, glass grinders, glass-cutting tools, and more

Delta Porter Cable (deltaportercable.com)
Power tools, saws, and belt sanders

Fire Mountain Gems and Beads (firemountaingems.com)
Jewelry findings, beads, supplies

Green Glass Cast (greenglasscast.com)
Glass casting kits and molds

Lortone (lortone.com)
Lapidary and jewelry equipment, rock tumblers, polishers

Crafted Findings (craftedfindings.com)
Rivet Piercing/Setting Tool, jewelry-making supplies, punch tool, eyelets, rivets

Metal Clay Supply (metalclaysupply.com)
Ring mandrel, Lilly Kiln, jewelry-making supplies

Mosaic mercantile (mosaicmercantile.com)
Tile nippers

Objects and Elements (objectsandelements.com)
Ice Resin, bezels, ring blanks

Paperclay (paperclay.com)
Air-hardening clay

Plaid Enterprises (plaidonline.com)
Mod Podge® decoupage glue

Rio Grande (riogrande.com)
Jewelry-making tools, supplies, findings, patina solution

Sherri Haab Shop (sherrihaab-shop.com)
Craft and jewelry-making supplies, ring bezel blanks, resin clay, books, DVDs

Sizzix (sizzix.com)
Sizzix Big shot Shape Cutting Machine, dies, cutters, tools, accessories

Tandy Leather Factory (tandyleatherfactory.com)
Leather, leathercraft tools

Toner Crafts (tonercrafts.com)
Weave Wheel

UGotGlass? (ugotglass.com)
Glass, fusing supplies, molds, tools

Vintaj Natural Brass (vintaj.com)
Arte Metal Decorivets, jewelry findings, metal stampings, embellishments

Volcano Arts (volcanoarts.biz)
Eyelets, metal tools, findings, craft supplies

Weisser Glass Studio (weisserglass.com)
Glass supplies, molds, kiln wash, sanding and cutting supplies for glass

We R Memory Keepers (weronthenet.com)
Crop-A-Dile punch and eyelet setter, eyelets

Black and White T-Shirt Rose Necklace by Michelle Haab.

Index